Energy Poverty Among Women in Jamaica's Low-Income Communities

Shinique Walters

Energy Poverty Among Women in Jamaica's Low-Income Communities

palgrave
macmillan

Shinique Walters
Department of Government
University of the West Indies, Mona
Kingston, Jamaica

ISBN 978-3-031-89078-9   ISBN 978-3-031-89079-6 (eBook)
https://doi.org/10.1007/978-3-031-89079-6

© The Editor(s) (if applicable) and The Author(s), under exclusive license to Springer Nature Switzerland AG 2025

This work is subject to copyright. All rights are solely and exclusively licensed by the Publisher, whether the whole or part of the material is concerned, specifically the rights of translation, reprinting, reuse of illustrations, recitation, broadcasting, reproduction on microfilms or in any other physical way, and transmission or information storage and retrieval, electronic adaptation, computer software, or by similar or dissimilar methodology now known or hereafter developed.
The use of general descriptive names, registered names, trademarks, service marks, etc. in this publication does not imply, even in the absence of a specific statement, that such names are exempt from the relevant protective laws and regulations and therefore free for general use.
The publisher, the authors and the editors are safe to assume that the advice and information in this book are believed to be true and accurate at the date of publication. Neither the publisher nor the authors or the editors give a warranty, expressed or implied, with respect to the material contained herein or for any errors or omissions that may have been made. The publisher remains neutral with regard to jurisdictional claims in published maps and institutional affiliations.

Cover image credit : Pattern © Melisa Hasan

This Palgrave Macmillan imprint is published by the registered company Springer Nature Switzerland AG.
The registered company address is: Gewerbestrasse 11, 6330 Cham, Switzerland

If disposing of this product, please recycle the paper.

Preface

This book looks at how gender dynamics intersect with energy access in low-income communities in Jamaica. Over the years, through research, conversations, and fieldwork, it became clear that women are central to sustainable solutions but are often overlooked in decision-making processes. In *Energy Poverty for Women in Communities, Jamaica*, I aim to shed light on these intersections and propose actionable solutions

Dedication – To my mother who thought me the need to work hard and to never give up. "In loving memory of my mother, Opal Davis (1960–2017), whose resilience and unwavering spirit illuminated our home even in the darkest moments. This book is dedicated to her and to every woman in low-income households who, despite limited resources, who has become a source of light, strength, and hope for their families."

To my daughter, Zindzi and Brother Sekou Let us always remain focused as I try to navigate and provide inspiration to combat poverty.

Kingston, Jamaica   Shinique Walters

Contents

1 **Introduction to the Concept of Gender and Energy Poverty**   1
    Introduction   2
    Low Income   2
    Energy Poverty   3
    Feminization of Poverty   3
    Care Economy   3
    Gender and Electricity in Communities   5
    Energy Poverty and Climate Change in Communities   6
    Rationale for Energy Poverty in Jamaica   7
    Gender and Energy Poverty   8
    Implications of Having Affordable and Accessible Energy on Low-Income Households in Jamaica   12
    Environmental Impacts   15
    Gender and Energy Poverty in the Caribbean   17
    Implication of Energy Poverty   18
    Energy Poverty and Gender   18
    Energy Poverty Affects Health and Environment   19
    Energy Poverty and Gender and Its Impact on Community Development   20
    Methodology   21
    References   22

2 Conceptual Framework 27
Feminist Political Ecology 29
Energy Justice 30
Gender and Development Theory 31
Social Reproduction Theory 33
Technology Adoption and Diffusion Theory 34
Participatory Approaches 35
Ecofeminism 36
Energy Democracy 38
References 39

3 The Impact of Energy Poverty on Gender 41
The Impact of Energy Poverty on Gender Particularly on Women in a Global Perspective 42
A Global Perspective of Energy Poverty 42
Global Finance of Energy Poverty 44
Innovative Technologies Globally 45
Impact of Energy Poverty on Women Globally 46
Women's Health and Its Impact by Energy Poverty 52
The Role of Energy Poverty and Education 53
Economic Opportunities and Energy Poverty 54
How Do We Encourage Energy and Promote Gender Equity? 54
Policy and Institutional Reforms 58
Capacity Building and Education 59
Public-Private Partnerships 59
References 60

4 Implications of Having Affordable and Accessible Energy on Low-Income Households 65
Economic Implications 66
Health Implications 68
Environmental Implications 68
Social Implications 69
Policy Implications 69
Renewable Energy Promotes Equity 71
References 73

5 Global Implication of Gender and Energy Poverty 75
Energy Poverty in the Caribbean 76
Gender Roles 77
Female-Headed Households and Businesses 82
Female-Headed Business 83
How Is the Caribbean Affected by Energy Poverty 84
Economic Impacts 85
Social Inequality 85
Health Risk 86
Environmental Impacts 86
Jamaica and Energy Poverty 87
Consequences of Energy Poverty in Jamaica 89
Social Consequences 90
Environmental Consequences 91
Health Consequences 92
The Impact of Energy Poverty on Youth, Disabled, and Minority Groups 93
Impact on Young Women 93
Impact on Disabled Women 94
Impact on Minority Groups 95
References 96

6 Recommendations 101
Recommendation to Improve Smarter Energy Sources 102
Education and Awareness 112
Financial Incentives 115
Regulation and Standards 116
Technology and Innovation 121
Encouraging Clean and Efficient Energy Consumption: Key Recommendations for Stakeholders 124
Conclusion 126
References 127

References 131

Index 149

List of Figures

Fig. 1.1	Kilometres travelled in the last 12 months for personal purpose included for transportation	14
Fig. 5.1	Represents the number of respondents who currently use the Services of JPS	87
Fig. 5.2	Represents the number of respondents who are happy with their JPS bill (monthly)	90
Fig. 6.1	Recommended areas to encourage clean energy	111
Fig. 6.2	Features suggested that should be part of a concept of energy poverty	114

CHAPTER 1

Introduction to the Concept of Gender and Energy Poverty

Abstract This introduction chapter provides an overview of what energy poverty is. It also conceptualizes the following terms: low-income households and energy poverty. The chapter also speaks to the approach to the feminisation of poverty, as women have the main responsibility within the household to care for the economy. The triple burden of women within their communities is also discussed. Women have the responsibility to care not just for her home and extended family but also look at the community needs. A quick overview is given of gender and electricity in the community and the impact that energy poverty has on climate change in Jamaica. Energy poverty also speaks to the general impact it has on women as the use of alternative forms of energy affect the daily sustenance of women and their families especially within Jamaica. The chapter also speaks to the challenges that energy has on women and the environment. The approach that was used to collect the data included an explanatory qualitative and quantitative technique, as this was important to describe the existing situation with women and electricity usage, as well as energy use, particularly at home.

Keywords Energy poverty • Feminization of poverty • Families and women and the environment

Introduction

Jamaica like any other country relies heavily on energy for the day-to-day needs of its citizens. With this reliance, various challenges have resulted in energy poverty being of concern. Individuals who do not have enough access to energy are deprived of necessities (light, cooking fuel). It deprives them of possibilities for holistic development by including women at all levels of the renewable energy value chain. Rose (2024) stated that it is thought to not just financially empower these women. The cost of energy in Jamaica as of March 2021 is US$0.307 per kWh for homes and US$0.248 per kWh for enterprises, encompassing all components of the electricity bill, such as power pricing, distribution, taxes, and returns (profits). Electricity use has increased significantly in recent years. This increase has caused many households to struggle to cope with the increase because of having to deal with the cost of obtaining power.

However, more women have been significantly impacted by the cost of electricity. This is since more Jamaican women operate in single-sex households and must manage the well-being of their children (Beckford, 2018). For Jamaican women, energy poverty leads to time poverty, which, according to Bishop (2022), is the chronic experience of having too many things to accomplish but not enough time to complete them. It prevents individuals from working, upgrading their skills, receiving an education, and adapting to and minimizing the effects of climate change. This is often due to the high cost of gaining access to electricity. To further understand, the following areas were conceptualized for this study:

Low Income

Most debates about energy poverty focus on low-income communities. These are frequently referred to as communities with little or no income to access societal resources such as money, property, medical care, or education. To establish an equal environment, governments subsidize these fundamental resources to ensure a standard of living for persons with lower-income levels (Jayaweera et al., 1989). Low-income housing, as defined in this document, is housing supplied to satisfy the requirements of Jamaicans with no or low income. In Jamaica, the poverty line determines lower-income levels. The poverty line serves as a benchmark for spending and resource access, with many impoverished people living just above or below the annual consumption poverty level of $J221,130.78 (Williams, 2006).

ENERGY POVERTY

For the purposes of this book, Reddy (2000) defines energy poverty as a situation in which individuals or communities lack access to inexpensive, reliable, and clean energy services, particularly electricity, that are necessary to meet their fundamental needs and improve overall well-being for themselves and their community's sustainability. Energy poverty affects marginalized populations, rural areas, and low-income households. The theory of energy poverty includes not only a lack of access to energy services, but also issues of price and reliability, acknowledging the problem's multifaceted nature by citizens (International Renewable Energy Agency, 2019).

FEMINIZATION OF POVERTY

According to Pearce and Standing (2001), the feminization of poverty refers to women bearing an inconsistent and increasing burden of poverty, particularly in comparison to men. It emphasizes the gendered character of poverty, with women being more likely to endure higher poverty rates and facing unique obstacles and disadvantages because of their gender. This phenomenon is driven by a variety of social, economic, and cultural factors, all of which contribute to gender disparities in income, resources, and opportunities. This has also resulted in another segment known as the care economy.

CARE ECONOMY

According to the European Institute for Gender Equality (2021), the "Care Economy" is the "part of human endeavor, both physical and social, that is concerned with the task of caring for the present and future workforce and the general population as a whole, including the domestic provisioning of food, clothing, and shelter." Furthermore, the Caribbean Policy Research Institute (CAPRI) (2023) described the care economy as paid care employment, unpaid care work conducted by family, friends/neighbours, or volunteers, and government investment in the care sector.

Furthermore, unpaid care provision is widely perceived as an endless, cost-free resource that fills gaps when governmental services are unavailable.

Latin American and Caribbean High-Level Panel Conference, Hon. Olivia Babsy Grange remarked, Globally, women and girls are responsible for 75% of unpaid care and domestic work in homes and communities daily. Furthermore, the International Labour Organisation (ILO) anticipates that women globally perform 4 hours and 25 minutes of unpaid care work daily, compared to 1 hour and 23 minutes for men (Jamaica Information Service, 2019). According to Grange (2021), the findings reveal that women suffer the most owing to inequities in care and are most likely to suffer due to increased trauma, overwork, and underpayment. They are also more likely to face sexual harassment and gender bias in the job.

Grange (2021) remarked, "The data indicate that women suffer the most due to the inequalities in care and are most likely to suffer due to increased trauma, being overworked and underpaid. They are also at risk of experiencing higher rates of sexual harassment and workplace gender biases."

However, according to the International Monetary Fund (2020), the COVID-19 pandemic has had a substantial impact on the Jamaican economy. Berik (2017) pointed out that despite the synergy between international financial institutions to promote gender equality leading to economic growth, a consistent, untouched gap in literature lingers; as they shun the ideology of the potential of gender wage inequality fostering growth and the macroeconomic enabling conditions for gender equality, which are also as a result of the lack of infrastructures that they place on having access to safe and inexpensive access to energy.

Evidently, the majority of women's productive time is spent on unpaid caregiving and nonproductive activities. In addition, women at all income levels perform more unpaid care work than males. Lower-income women, nevertheless, perform the majority of all women's unpaid care work. It is assumed that the time women spend doing unpaid care duties may be employed to do compensated productive employment. The results show that the economy of unpaid care work has a significant cost. Finally, the survey found that "Jamaican women bear the largest responsibility for unpaid reproductive work, while having less opportunity for resources and paid work than men." Women at all income levels do more unpaid caregiver work than males, with lower-income women doing the most, and the time women spend on unpaid care work is time that could have been spent on paid and productive labour (CAPRI, 2023). The report shows that Jamaican policymakers are concerned with increasing labour force participation and productivity in the pursuit of economic growth if they are concerned with the composition and quality of the future employees, and if they are concerned with the health and well-being of the entire society, whether as a means to overall greater productivity and economic growth or as an end in themselves, women's care needs must be addressed.

By measuring and monetizing unpaid care work, calculations may be performed to indicate the amount to which relieving women of the burden of unpaid care work can have an impact on the firm and the broader economy, informing applicable legislation. The report investigates several strategies to do this, including fiscal policy, governmental provision of/support for care services, and private sector provision of/support for employees' care requirements (The Gleaner, 2019).

However, the ravages made by COVID-19 have further exacerbated the issue of inequities and inequalities within the care economy. Moreover, the inequity reflects the representation of women and their rights being catered for. This includes equal pay for equal work done or simply being remunerated for unpaid care work that contributed significantly to the production levels of society. Furthermore, though COVID-19 presented great setbacks for the economy, the government of Jamaica was able to implement strategies to minimize the effects of COVID-19 on the poor and the vulnerable through its CARE programme, which sought to put money and food on the table of the most vulnerable in the population. In the end, the argument rests that gender equality will result in economic growth, and as such, the care economy must be at the forefront of policy considerations.

Gender and Electricity in Communities

From the study, the issue of gender and electricity access in Jamaican communities reveals the need for more targeted interventions to address disparities and promote gender equality. Many factors currently affect various communities regarding gender and the use of electricity. According to Beckford, 2018 as previously highlighted, women are predominantly responsible for household chores and caregiving, which require reliable access to electricity for cooking, lighting, and operating household appliances. However, they are faced with the issue of limited decision-making power and financial resources that may hinder women's ability to secure reliable electricity services based on the gendered division of labour and has contributed to further disparities in electricity access between men and women within communities. The intersection of gender and income intensifies energy poverty among women, creating barriers to their economic empowerment and overall well-being (Gibson & Dyer, 2018).

Additionally, gender education and the digital divide are crucial to women's sustainability in these communities, as access to electricity is crucial for educational opportunities, particularly in the digital age. Lack of electricity access can also hinder students' ability to study at night or utilize digital learning tools, exacerbating existing gender inequalities in education as is often shared by persons residing in rural communities. This can further hamper their access to additional schooling with the passing of an examination. Therefore, we must examine the various areas to bridge the digital divide while ensuring equitable electricity access to enhance educational opportunities for all genders within their communities (CAPRI, 2021).

Energy Poverty and Climate Change in Communities

Climate change and the consequences of energy poverty are significant challenges that women face. Rural women, who are largely responsible for food and energy security, rely heavily on locally available natural resources. Climate change offers substantial obstacles to sustainable development around the world. Therefore, a link exists between energy poverty and climate change in communities. The study also investigates the implications for climate vulnerability, including increasing sea levels, increased hurricane frequency and intensity, and shifting rainfall patterns. These considerations include additional challenges for energy-poor communities, as disruptions in energy supply and infrastructure impede their ability to cope with and recover from climate-related catastrophes. Vulnerable groups are disproportionately affected, with prolonged energy insecurity and increased exposure to climate threats (Campbell, 2016).

Furthermore, there is a greater need to promote sustainability within neighbourhoods by encouraging the use of solar, wind, and hydroelectric technologies that can provide clean and reliable energy while lowering greenhouse gas emissions, particularly in communities with the resources to do so. Implementing energy efficiency measures in houses and appliances can reduce energy demand and expenditures, which speaks to the financial resources of women in these areas (MSET, 2019).

To tackle energy poverty and global warming in Jamaican communities, an integrated and comprehensive strategy is required that promotes renewable energy options, improves energy efficiency, and strengthens climate resilience. Second, improving climate resilience through infrastructure improvements and community-based initiatives can help communities withstand and recover from events associated with climate change (MSET, 2019), while also creating a more sustainable and equitable future for Jamaican communities that promotes energy access, poverty reduction, and climate resilience.

RATIONALE FOR ENERGY POVERTY IN JAMAICA

Despite numerous definitions of energy poverty, all allude to a degree of energy utilization that is lacking to meet certain basic needs. According to Winkler et al. (2011), "energy poverty may be defined by the following underlying indicators: the absence of sufficient choice in accessing adequate, affordable, reliable, quality, safe and environmentally sound energy services to support development." Furthermore, Kaygusuz (2011) asserts that energy poverty is mainly concentrated in the developing world, predominantly in South Asia and Africa, where it manifests itself through reliance on conventional sources of energy such as biomass and the absence of access to clean and safe fuels. It is no secret that wealthier countries often possess numerous sources compared to poorer countries, especially rural areas, where there are limited resources or none. Thus, the most utilized energy source in poorer countries is wood.

Energy is one of the most basic contributions to supporting individuals' livelihoods. Energy allows for the provision of boiled water, warmth, and cooked food at its most fundamental level. Using biomass as an energy carrier for poor people has long been established. According to Eckholm (1975), while the world was still suffering from the international oil crisis, the other energy crisis was brought to the fore by the World Resources Institute in 1975. The World Bank (1996) asserted that even though biomass fuels are utilized by two billion people, there has not been much attempt to analyse energy poverty in depth.

The utilization of biomass possesses numerous consequences for less fortunate people. The fuel quality is low, and when burned, it emits particles and smoke that can negatively affect one's health. The hours spent on fuel collection means that other livelihood activities cannot be completed. According to Reddy (2000), although almost all families in rural areas will utilize biomass as an energy carrier, less fortunate households spend more time in the pursuit of more biomass fuel than higher-income households. Furthermore, ESMAP (1999) asserts that higher-income households will buy other fuels of higher quality and have numerous uses than poorer households. In urban areas, less fortunate people spend much of their income on cooking fuels than higher-income households. Furthermore, Barnes (1995) asserts that poor families in urban areas spend approximately 20% of their income on fuel. While in rural areas, poor households impose restrictions on their fuel purchases for only lighting purposes such as kerosene and candles.

Even though the utilization of energy carriers is complicated, wealthier households may have options to choose from in terms of their energy carrier, which often results in them opting for more efficient and cleaner "modern" energy carriers of gas or electricity. Wealthy households often combine traditional and modern fuels for a particular purpose. Similarly, modern energy carriers are not characterized by negative time and health effects like biomass. Thus, well-off people possess the capabilities to purchase appliances required to utilize modern energy carriers. When these households rely heavily on biomass fuels, more fuel-efficient stoves are purchased to help keep costs down. It helps save a significant amount of money per unit of energy consumed. Reddy and Reddy (1994) are of the notion that less fortunate households cannot invest in such appliances, rather choosing options that are cheaply priced since they lack the capital needed. The consequences for the poor are that resources are utilized for low-quality fuels and are then utilized at low efficiency, ultimately reducing their ability to garner the financial resources necessary to invest.

Gender and Energy Poverty

According to Denton (2001), "gender refers to different social roles that women and men play, and the power relations between them. Gender relations influence how communities, households, and institutions are organised, how decisions are made, and how resources are used." Thus, to comprehend the effects gender activities have on the environment, men and women's responsibilities, roles, control and access over resources must be analysed. Similarly, understanding the intricacies of men and women's relationships with the environment plays a critical role in the development of solutions and addressing issues for more sustainable utilization of energy resources. By omitting gender, it distorts one's understanding of the impact humans have on the environment in its entirety.

Recently, an emergence of a complex understanding of the energy and gender relationship has begun. Currently, debates on this discourse put forward the notion that productive activities requiring energy inputs must have the involvement of both women and men. Even though household energy burdens remain predominantly the responsibilities of women, accessing modern energy carriers such as electricity and clean fuels affects both women and men. The distinction in the debate stems from the fact that energy services available affect women and men differently based on what energy applications they require and are involved in. However, most debates on legislative framework and energy policy have opted for a gender blind or gender-neutral stance with regard to energy technology, rural energy policy, and energy pricing.

Therefore, policies relating to energy often fail because they are not cognizant of the assets and needs of men and women. Huyer and Westholme (2001) are of the notion that a partial explanation can be inferred from the fact that in rural areas biomass can be collected at no cost mainly by children and women, so it is not included within national energy accounts which renders the issue invisible. Due to energy-poverty issues being considered "invisible" it results in decision-makers being partially unaware of their impact thus, strategies and policies result in failure because they do not successfully address the problem in its entirety.

According to Gunningham (2013), there has been a significant amount of policy and academic attention on energy poverty in the Global South due to the broad effects on health and well-being. From a production perspective, women's participation within the energy sector is largely restricted to biomass management and forestry in rural areas, while in urban areas, women remain the victims of environmental impacts of coal-based electricity production that is utilized by middle to upper groups. During the formulation of energy policy, only a few women are involved while projects concerning big energy have been reserved for men. Households often resort to open fires which may lead to increased levels of air pollution due to a lack of access to modern fuels within the home. González-Eguino (2015) asserts that an estimated 1.3 million people, predominantly women and children, die from smoke and fumes from open fires per year. Furthermore, because of these circumstances there are significant consequences on income, labour productivity, household time budgets, and personal safety (Elias & Victor, 2005).

Thus, energy poverty is a problem that is "highly gendered" due to women being the ones to bear the brunt of all consequences associated with a lack of energy access while having to suffer from systemic discrimination. Furthermore, women are far more disadvantaged than men because their control and access to resources such as credit, cash, and land is more limited than that of men. Similarly, the technical skills that women possess are often considered less than the skills that men possess because when compared to men their experiences with male dominated equipment and hardware is limited. The inference can be drawn that when formulating energy interventions to aid individuals achieve mobility to move away from poverty, there are restrictions to women's abilities to respond.

According to Denton (2002), when gender is included, 70% of the 1.3 billion people in developing nations living below the poverty line are women. Similarly, the vast majority of the 2 billion people who do not have access to modern energy services live in rural areas, with women leading most poor homes. Girls and women are more impacted by a lack of modern fuels than males are. Millions of girls and women allocate up to eight hours per day carrying dung, fuel wood, and other conventional biofuels. In situations where fuel resources are few, households frequently confront substantial difficulty in achieving their basic energy requirements. This scarcity can lead to tough resource allocation decisions within homes, with a particular impact on children's education. Research suggests that during such situations, families may prioritize immediate survival demands above long-term educational commitments. Modi et al. (2005) identifies an important trend: as energy supplies become scarce, girl children are disproportionately excluded from educational institutions.

This decision is usually motivated by the necessity for extra hands to help gather fuel or conduct other home duties that support the family's energy needs. Girls' education is frequently neglected in favour of family obligations. The repercussions of this withdrawal are significant. Without access to education, these girls grow up lacking critical literacy skills and knowledge that may empower and improve their prospects. A lack of education not only hinders their personal growth, but also their ability to actively participate in economic activities later in life.

In almost all instances the energy problem for the poor is "we do not have it." But this issue is even worse for girls and women because of a lack of control, access, social dynamics, and power relations. Women and men in a society are ascribed different aspirations, roles and needs for energy. Furthermore, the gender dimension of poverty and energy makes its appearance in numerous ways. Take for instance households with adult women and men present, the division of labour is highly gendered with women being allocated household energy provision responsibilities in relation to the influence they wield within the household, especially in the kitchen. Dutta et al. (2017) is of the notion that women are largely confined to gendered spaces such as the home and more specifically the kitchen which one can consider an amalgamation of their work and social spaces. Furthermore, as it relates to energy, the emergence of gendered spaces has resulted in these spaces being considered crucial leveraging areas when making decisions such as on income-generation, health, and new technologies.

Makan (1995) posits that in situations where energy purchases are necessary, men typically assume the role of decision-makers, particularly evident in the acquisition of batteries for radios. He further observed that a study conducted in South Africa revealed significant spending on batteries by young men for the purpose of enjoying music. However, it was often the case that female household members had little to no influence over these battery purchases and were frequently denied access to the devices themselves. Additionally, in various households, items deemed "recreational," such as radios and televisions, were prioritized for purchase before considering equipment that could alleviate the time and effort required for domestic tasks. Consequently, decisions regarding what to buy and who has ownership of these items are predominantly made by male members of the family.

Abdourahman (2010) emphasizes that the unequal distribution of time between men and women, both in the economic sphere and within domestic settings, adversely affects women's access to their economic rights. This disparity is rooted in patriarchal structures prevalent in numerous cultural systems. Abdourahman argues that due to this patriarchal dominance, women are often assigned roles and responsibilities that are not only time-consuming but also excessively burdensome. However, unlike their male counterparts, women are frequently deprived of the necessary energy and resources to effectively manage these responsibilities. In essence, the imbalance in time allocation creates a cycle where women's potential for economic empowerment is stifled. The societal expectation for women to fulfil extensive household duties limits their opportunities for participation in the workforce or pursuing personal development. Consequently, this leads to a systemic disadvantage that perpetuates gender inequality within both economic and social frameworks.

Rengasamy et al. (2001) provide a case study of a rural electrification initiative in Tamil Nadu, highlighting that men were the primary beneficiaries of this development. The introduction of electricity facilitated the use of irrigation pumps, which replaced traditional oxen-drawn water systems. This shift was significant because managing oxen had traditionally been a male responsibility. With the advent of irrigation pumps, men found themselves with increased leisure time, which they could then allocate to enhancing their agricultural practices and engaging more actively in political affairs. This newfound time contributed to an enhancement of their human and social capital. On the other hand, women did not gain the same advantages from the electrification initiative. Their needs were not satisfied because the electricity did not take the place of their current obligations. Because of the changes brought about by electricity, women remained to bear the customary burdens without any relief, while males benefitted from expanded prospects for personal and professional development.

Implications of Having Affordable and Accessible Energy on Low-Income Households in Jamaica

The reality of many homes in developing nations is the use of biomass—waste material, dung, coal, and wood—for cooking and heating. In homes, biomass fuels are frequently used in clay, brick, or metal cookers. Furthermore, the illumination needs are fulfilled primarily using candles and occasionally by kerosene lamps. Although this kind of energy enables households to meet their fundamental necessities, the high level of pollution it produces has significant negative consequences on health. Inefficient combustion and inadequate ventilation in dwellings are the main causes of this pollution. Moreover, elevated carbon monoxide levels, aromatic compounds, and suspended particles define this kind of pollution. About 20% of Jamaican homes do not have access to inexpensive, dependable energy.

Since many Jamaicans live in rural areas and rely on wood or charcoal for cooking, this condition has had a negative impact on many aspects of life, including health. Such behaviours may aggravate respiratory conditions like asthma. In addition, food preservation is made more difficult by the lack of electricity, which increases the danger of foodborne infections. Hendrick et al. (2023) shows that students struggle to do their assignments, participate in class projects, and stay in touch with their lecturers. During the COVID-19 pandemic, when many students had trouble charging their devices, this problem became more apparent.

Jessel et al. (2019) indicates that certain individuals rely on ductless hot air units and unvented gas heaters as their primary sources of heat. Due to their residence in low-income households, they lack the financial means to make necessary improvements to their heating infrastructure. The use of these heating methods is linked to various health issues, including allergies, respiratory symptoms, cognitive impairments, and throat irritation. These problems arise from elevated levels of nitrogen dioxide and volatile organic compounds present in the environment. Additionally, utilizing these heaters as alternative heating solutions poses risks such as fire hazards, injuries, and even fatalities. This array of challenges is referred to as thermal stress. Jessel et al. (2019) defines thermal stress as a condition experienced by individuals and families who cannot adequately or consistently heat or cool their homes due to financial constraints related to utility bills or limited access to sufficient services.

People who experience energy poverty are more likely to turn to coping mechanisms, such as cutting back on their use of energy sources or adopting drastic energy-saving techniques to lower their overall energy costs. One instance of this is when people don't use their refrigerators, which reduces the amount of fresh food they can eat. Families that avoid using warm water can also be at risk for illnesses due to poor cleanliness. Some turn to using dim lighting, which can cause eye strain and worsen headaches and migraines. There are two types of thermal stress: heat stress and cold stress.

Oliveras et al. (2020) claims that respiratory and cardiovascular disorders are associated with cold temperatures. In addition to impairing immunity, cold exposure can increase a person's vulnerability to infections and respiratory illnesses like the flu and cold. Moreover, living in energy poverty in colder climates might raise a child's risk of respiratory problems considerably. According to Jessel et al. (2019), cold stress increases the incidence of heart attacks and strokes in people with a diagnosis of cardiovascular disease. Furthermore, research indicates that residences with insufficient heating often have worsening arthritis symptoms. The heightened mortality rate among individuals with Alzheimer's disease can be attributed to behavioural and physiological reactions brought on by cold stress.

Furthermore, Sangha et al. (2020) has shown that symptoms of arthritis exacerbate in households with insufficient warmth. Individuals with Alzheimer's disease have a greater death rate as a result of cold stress-induced behavioural and physiological reactions. Cold stress has a similar impact on teenage health; research shows that the prevalence of pneumonia and other diseases increases among youngsters with impaired immune systems. Cold weather exacerbates respiratory problems including coughing and wheezing, lowering overall quality of life.

Jessel et al. (2019) states that heat stress is defined by the inability of households to afford or obtain energy necessary for cooling their living spaces. The health consequences associated with heat stress include cardiovascular problems such as heat strokes, hypertension, heart attacks, strokes, dehydration, and hyperthermia. Furthermore, the risk of acute renal failure also rises with increased heat stress. Additionally, sleep disturbances caused by heat stress can worsen existing mental health issues. Families attempting to mitigate heat stress by opening windows and doors to facilitate the escape of heat inadvertently expose themselves to outdoor air pollutants. This exposure includes emissions from motor vehicles, which are linked to respiratory illness symptoms (Fig. 1.1).

The bar graph above shows that majority of the respondents for the year used less than 5000 kilometres for personal purpose included for transportation. One of the most obvious advantages of limiting mobility to less than 5000 kilometres per year is a significant decrease in fuel use. Vehicles use fossil fuels, releasing greenhouse gases and other pollutants into the environment. Individuals can reduce their fuel consumption

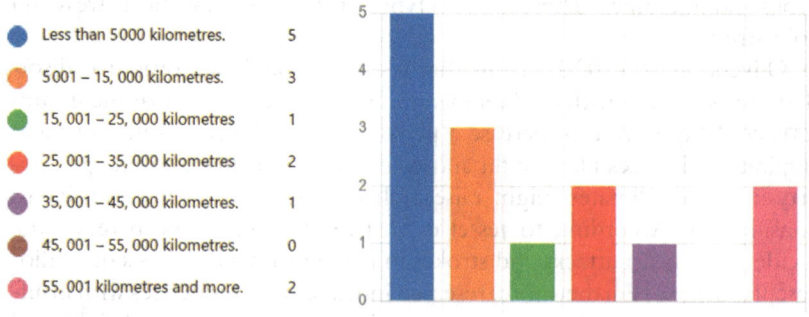

Fig. 1.1 Kilometres travelled in the last 12 months for personal purpose included for transportation

significantly by driving fewer kilometres (Pei, 2021). For example, if an average car uses 8 litres of fuel every 100 kilometres, cutting travel from 15,000 kilometres to 5000 kilometres might save around 800 litres of gasoline per year. This not only saves energy, but also decreases reliance on fossil fuels.

Apart from physical and physiological health effects, energy poverty can lead to mental health issues. Robinson (2019) proclaims that energy poverty is more likely to impact the mental health of women. Qualitative research showed that women living in poverty who have children and other dependants feel stressed, chronically exhausted, and tired. Oliveras et al. (2020) asserts that energy poverty is typically associated with household financial debt and housing insecurity which can both worsen mental health. Additionally, energy poverty impairs children's emotional well-being, educational fulfilment, and increases their risk of having accidents and injuries at home.

In addition to the physical and physiological health effects, energy poverty can lead to mental health issues. Robinson (2019) notes that the mental health repercussions of energy poverty are more pronounced for women than for men. Qualitative studies indicate that women living in poverty with children and other dependants often face stress, chronic fatigue, and exhaustion. Oliveras et al. (2020) highlights that energy poverty is frequently associated with household financial debt and housing instability, both of which can adversely affect mental health. Moreover, energy poverty negatively influences children's emotional well-being, academic performance, and increases their risk of accidents and injuries at home.

Environmental Impacts

Like many Caribbean countries, Jamaicans have been classified as a warm environment, particularly during the summer months. Families that do not have access to power may struggle to stay cool, disrupting their sleep and making it difficult for them to focus. Along with this comes fewer economic options, as a lack of electricity has forced low-income households to develop their own enterprises or work from home. This might make it difficult for families to save money for other expenses like food and rent.

With all the obstacles mentioned above, an increase in safe, economical, and dependable access to electricity can help enhance access to better health conditions by lowering the risk of respiratory disorders such as asthma. Secondly, having access to power may make it easier to keep food chilled, lowering the risk of foodborne illness. Increased access to electricity can also assist students perform their schoolwork, research projects, and keep connected with their teachers and peers. Additionally, access to electricity could make it easier for families to stay cool during hot weather, which could improve their ability to learn and for families to be better able to allocate finances to other sectors for the home. These factors would all help to improve the health, education, and economic opportunities. Governments and businesses should work together to make affordable and accessible energy a reality for all Jamaicans.

The link between the environment and energy poverty is due to land use change. Traditional biomass serves as the primary source of energy for the impoverished. According to Guruswamy (2011), these fires are caused by the combustion of wood, raw coal, animal dung, crop waste, other residues, and hazardous biomass. However, overexploitation causes increased land degradation, deforestation, and desertification. The reliance on trees as a fuel source increases pressure on forests around the world, particularly in areas where energy poverty exists and demand for trees exceeds natural supply through regrowth. UNDP (Breaking up with Fossil Fuels, 2017) asserts that burning wood in open fires has significantly increased global warming effects. However, most solid traditionally used fuels, excluding coal, are renewable. This is because trees can be replanted. The underlying assumption for this statement is that most of the energy needed is used for heating or cooking. Therefore, it is likely to be sourced from trees or agricultural crop waste which can both be labelled as carbon neutral.

Ensari (2017) explores different views, one of which states that energy poverty has led to environmental depletion and if energy poverty is further prolonged in specific regions, their air quality will be poor, and their forests will continuously be depleted. Energy poverty is a multidimensional issue. Another view that was explored shows that energy poverty's effect on the environment is indirectly proportional to income. Therefore, lower-income families and individuals experiencing energy poverty affect the environment less than higher-income families and individuals who have more access and availability to energy sources. The level of income and greenhouse gas emissions is positively associated. Low-income individuals and families emit less greenhouse gases whereas middle- and high-income families and individuals emit more greenhouse gases from energy use. However, this type of correlation may not be applied to every type of consumption.

Consequently, Guruswamy (2011) attests that emissions from the burning of biomass are a significant cause of black carbon, which in turn increases global warming. The black carbon emitted by burning biomass, such as coal, is currently the second largest contributor to global warming after carbon dioxide emissions that arise from practices such as deforestation. Notably, black carbon warms the atmosphere at a higher rate than greenhouse gases like methane. Both black carbon and greenhouse gases contribute to atmospheric warming, which facilitates the absorption of both direct and reflected solar radiation. Furthermore, the presence of overlying black carbon on polar ice caps may lead to increased heat retention in the ice, resulting in accelerated melting and further exacerbating global warming.

Gender and Energy Poverty in the Caribbean

Energy poverty is present in the Caribbean region especially in rural areas of each country. Biomass such as trees and crop waste are readily available, and poverty is widespread in many countries. Jimenez et al. (2021) proclaims that more than 50% of rural households rely on biomass or kerosene for lighting. Overall, in Latin American countries, one in ten households spends over 20% of their income on energy. This affirms the level of energy poverty amongst Latin-American families. In contrast, 20% of the higher-income households have energy budgets as low as 1 to 4%. In higher-income families, the majority, about 70% of the 1 to 4% energy budget is spent towards fuel for travelling, whereas in low-income families, most of the energy budget is spent on electricity and food.

The presence of these differences therefore leads to disproportionate effects on fuel price changes. Increases in gasoline prices affect higher-income households more, whereas increases in domestic gas prices affect lower-income households more. An example is a 20% increase in gasoline prices would create energy expense increases equivalent to 0.2% in the lower-income families and a 0.88% in the highest. In contrast, a 20% increase in the price of domestic gas prices would lead to a 1.48% increase in energy costs for the lower-income households but only a 0.6% increase in energy costs for the higher-income households.

Implication of Energy Poverty

Energy availability determines how food is grown and cooked, the health and environmental impacts of how food is cooked, and how living spaces are kept cool or warm amongst other things. Martins et al. (2021) affirms that energy availability affects the lives of low-income families as they spend much of their time doing energy-related activities and much of their income to gain energy for basic needs. Over two billion people across the world are unable to access safe and clean energy sources and therefore resort to traditional biomass burning such as coal, wood, animal waste, and agriculture residue. Poverty in essence is the absence of certain basic abilities to function.

Energy poverty in general has multidimensional impacts on one's health, the environment, socialization, and cultural deprivations. For example, energy poverty consumes a person's time and labour which can negatively impact their health, deplete the environment of trees, and limit a person's capacities socially. Therefore, energy and poverty relations are hierarchical and link to multiple deprivations especially those related to health and social well-being. In Nepal, 86% of the energy is sourced from biomass which leads to a greater impact on the country's economic, health, sociocultural, and environmental aspects (Xiao et al., 2021)

Energy Poverty and Gender

Jamaica is affected by poverty just as other countries in the Caribbean. Jamaica Gleaner (2019) proclaims that in 2017, 14.5% of the Jamaican population is below the poverty line based on the international poverty threshold of earning US$1.90/day. At the current poverty threshold level, those Jamaicans below the poverty line cannot afford to pay for electricity and therefore will not pay for electricity. Many people resort to using biomass, but others find ways to steal electricity to solve their energy poverty.

Energy poverty has more of a negative impact on women than men. It is therefore necessary to focus on gender when examining energy poverty. As stated by Martins et al. (2021) "the studying of gender and energy poverty invites a human face that concerns equality and equities rather than growth and efficiency." Collecting wood for burning can take up to 20 hours a week and women can travel over difficult terrains to source the fuelwood. For example, in Nepal it has been estimated that women can walk over 20 kilometres per journey in search of fuelwood.

Women therefore tend to suffer from back problems from walking these long distances for many hours and carrying heavy loads of wood on their head. There are also lesser-known threats of rape and beatings, which contribute to the disproportionate burden of energy poverty on women compared to men. Children are also disadvantaged since they are frequently kept out of school to help their mother's collect firewood. This has a significant negative influence on the development and well-being of lower-income households (Ho et al., 2021).

The problem of energy poverty is not the lack of biomass energy but instead the lack of women's time and labour to manage their household energy due to the existing cultural values in addition to seeking biomass energy. Martins et al. (2021) states that women in rural areas of Nepal spend most of their time and labour on achieving the well-being of their family. Even though women are the main producers and managers of biomass energy in their homes especially in rural areas, they have limited access to the decision-making processes regarding any large-scale energy decisions.

ENERGY POVERTY AFFECTS HEALTH AND ENVIRONMENT

Due to the disproportionate effects of energy poverty on women, the health effects are therefore disproportional for women as well. In many cases, women in rural Nepal experience uterine prolapse which is attributed to carrying heavy fuelwood. Additionally, women often face the risk of miscarriages with high stress levels and heavy workload. Apart from collecting the biomass, using it can have major health effects. Martins et al. (2021) proclaims that a study in Nepal indicates that the highest percentage of infant mortality is associated with indoor air pollution caused by using traditional biomass. Women from the lowest-income households are unable to boil water to drink and eat less cooked food which heightens their health problems. These same health problems limit a woman's ability to participate in social activities, thereby affecting mental health.

In terms of environmental impacts, burning of biomass increases domestic air pollution, and decreases the productive capacity of land. Cutting down trees for biomass energy causes depletion of forest. This negatively impacts biodiversity through the extinction of natural species. Since trees act as carbon sinks, when they are cut down this releases carbon into the atmosphere which increases the level of greenhouse gases in the atmosphere. Soil quality can become degraded due to the uses of biomass from farm to fire. The degradation of soil quality is a major cause of food insecurity in the world. Martins et al. (2021) asserts that rural populations in poor countries pay the highest price for environmental degradation. This is because low-income rural families depend on various ecosystems to generate water, wood and other biomass. Forests are needed as they recycle nutrients, prevent soil erosion, act as a carbon sink, and replenish the soil quality.

Energy Poverty and Gender and Its Impact on Community Development

Munien and Ahmed (2012) posited in their study "A gendered perspective on energy poverty and livelihoods—Advancing the Millennium Development Goals in developing countries" that the gender dimensions of poverty were largely driven by feminist research and advocacy that challenged poverty assessments and policy's "gender blindness." Furthermore, Munien and Ahmed (2012) proposed the assumption that feminizing poverty (the feminization of poverty) drew attention to economic disparities between men and women, where women are underrepresented in development programmes, and the role of technology in filling that gap.

Chant (2003) also stated in her study "New contributions to the analysis of poverty: methodological and conceptual challenges to understanding poverty from a gender perspective," that these biases are visible in gender-based inequalities, which resulted from the interaction of material poverty and gender-based discrimination: as women face higher poverty burdens, income inequality, and unequal access to economic opportunities on the one hand. Furthermore, Munien and Ahmed stated that gender biases manifest spatially in men's and women's socialization and labour. Gendered spaces are said to limit women mostly to the private domains of the kitchen and house, which integrate their social and working environments. As a result, gendered spaces have arisen as crucial leverage areas for health, new technology, income-generating activities, and the need for energy-efficient and secure public places for women.

Rodgers (2022) said in their paper "Time Poverty: Conceptualization, Gender Differences, and Policy Implications" that time poverty is another contributing cause to women's poverty. Furthermore, they claimed that it is a gendered issue, with more women than men being labelled time deprived. Munien and Ahmed (2012) defined time poverty as the uneven allocation of time between men and women in the home and economy, which impedes women's access to economic opportunities. One may therefore argue that women's lack of economic rights will eventually limit their capacity to buy energy. They also stated that in many patriarchal cultural systems, women are allocated essential and time-consuming obligations that overburden them in the reproduction, production, family, and community sectors compared to their male counterparts. As a result, one might conclude that an increase in female-headed families positions women among the "poorest of the poor," since they are more likely to be poor and experience higher poverty levels than males.

Another point to consider is that women spend a significant amount of time on unpaid work, which restricts their ability to engage in other activities. Women generally have a heavier overall workload than men, performing a disproportionate amount of unpaid care and domestic tasks (Rodgers, 2022). Additionally, factors such as forced labour migration, marital breakdowns due to financial stress, and lack of formal marriage further contribute to women's poverty. Constrained by their multiple roles (productive, reproductive, and community engagement), women face labour market discrimination and are unable to benefit from a "dual earner" status as single breadwinners, which could help alleviate the pressures of neoliberal economic restructuring. As a result, female-headed households are more likely to experience poverty.

Moreover, the rise in women's involvement in informal work and casual labour adds complexity, as these job structures are marked by income and employment instability, gender inequalities in job status and pay, and a lack of benefits (Munien & Ahmed, 2012). The importance of women's participation in economic decision-making was highlighted. It was assumed that the women involved had access to and control over financial resources and their own labour. However, this assumption needed to consider the fragmented nature of women's work, which is often integrated with other activities.

Methodology

The book employed an explanatory technique to describe the existing situation with women and electricity usage, as well as energy use, particularly at home. The researchers also utilized a mixed-method approach as their methodology. It allowed for both quantitative and qualitative research. To conduct this study, the researcher used a stratified sample strategy to obtain 246 female participants. These females were engaged since it explained how electricity and other energy sources benefitted them in their daily lives, as well as how to use these different energy sources. Qualitatively, the study used the grounded theory research approach, which allowed us to create theories about the usage of energy by females in Jamaica.

To accomplish this, I conducted an interview with members of the energy sector to understand the use of energy in Jamaica, as well as a desk review to understand any policies and programme notes that we use when attempting to assess the use of energy by females within communities. Gender and Electricity is a concept that focuses on access to energy and gender equality in its acquisition. More importantly, not just mere access to clean energy but affordable and sustainable energy. As having access does not adequately consider the local social context and household power dynamics that exist.

References

Abdourahman, O. I. (2010). Time poverty: A contributor to women's poverty? *The African Statistical Journal, 11,* 1–22.

Barnes, D. F. (1995). Consequences of energy policies for the urban poor. *Energy Policy, 23*(9), 739–750.

Barrett, J. (2019, October 10). 50m reasons why - Reid, Pinnock, three others charged in ministry, CMU fraud. *The Gleaner.* https://jamaica-gleaner.com/article/lead-stories/20191010/50m-reasons-why-reid-pinnock-three-others-charged-ministry-cmu-fraud#google_vignette

Beckford, M. (2018). *Study underway to select local crops for biofuel production.* Jamaica Observer. https://advancedbiofuelsusa.info/tag/jamaica

Berik, G. (2017). *Toward more inclusive measures of economic well-being.* International Labour Organization. https://www.ilo.org/sites/default/files/wcmsp5/groups/public/@dgreports/@cabinet/documents/publication/wcms_649127.pdf

Bishop, H. (2022). *Custos Rotulorum of saint James, Jamaica.* https://www.custosofstjamesja.com/

Campbell, A. (2016). Price and income elasticities of electricity demand: Evidence from Jamaica. *Energy Economics, 56,* 1–10.

CAPRI. (2023, February 1). *Fair pay: The wage gap barrier to women's empowerment.* Caribbean Policy Research Institute (CAPRI). https://capricaribbean.org/document/fair-pay-wage-gap-barrier-womens-empowerment#:~:text=Women%20are%20still%20generally%20poorer,is%20the%20gender%20wage%20gap

Caribbean Policy Research Institute (CAPRI). (2021). *The real cost of unpaid care and domestic work*. https://www.capricaribbean.org/sites/default/files/documents/whocarestherealcostofunpaidcareanddomesticwork.pdf

Chant, S. (2003). *The 'engendering' of poverty analysis in developing regions: Progress since the United Nations Decade for Women, and priorities for the future* (New Working Paper Series No. 11). Gender Institute, London School of Economics and Political Science. http://eprints.lse.ac.uk/573/

Denton, F. (2001). Gendered impacts of climate change: A human security issue. *Energy Policy, 39*(6), 1037–1046.

Denton, F. (2002). Climate change vulnerability, impacts, and adaptation: Why does gender matter? *Gender & Development, 10*(2), 10–20.

Dutta, S., Kooijman, A., & Cecelski, E. (2017). *Energy access and gender: Getting the right balance*. ENERGIA, International Network on Gender and Sustainable Energy. https://www.energia.org/cm2/wp-content/uploads/2016/06/ENERGIA-news-16.pdf

Eckholm, E. (1975). *The other energy crisis: Firewood*. Worldwatch Paper 1.

Elias, R. J., & Victor, D. G. (2005). *Energy transitions in developing countries: A review of concepts and literature* (Working Paper No. 40). Program on Energy and Sustainable Development, Stanford University.

Energy Sector Management Assistance Programme (ESMAP). (1999). *Energy services for the world's poor*. World Bank.

Ensari, M. Ş. (2017). A study on the differences of entrepreneurship potential among generations. *Research Journal of Business and Management, 4*, 52–62. https://doi.org/10.17261/Pressacademia.2017.370

European Parliament. (2021, June). Gender equality: Economic value of care from the perspective. https://www.europarl.europa.eu/RegData/etudes/STUD/2021/694784/IPOL_STU(2021)694784_EN.pdf

Gibson, V., & Dyer, J. (2018). Project Juno: Advancing gender equality in physics careers in higher education in the United Kingdom. *Proceedings of Science, 314*, 555. https://doi.org/10.22323/1.314.0555

González-Eguino, M. (2015). Energy poverty: An overview. *Renewable and Sustainable Energy Reviews, 47*, 377–385.

Gunningham, N. (2013). Managing the energy trilemma: The case of Indonesia. *Energy Policy, 54*, 184–193.

Guruswamy, L. (2011). Energy poverty. *Annual Review of Environment and Resources, 36*(1), 139–161. https://doi.org/10.1146/annurev-environ-040610-090118

Hendrick, L., Opdenakker, M. C., & Van der Vaart, W. (2023). Students' academic engagement during COVID-19 times: A mixed-methods study into relatedness and loneliness during the pandemic. *Frontiers in Psychology, 14*, 1221003. https://doi.org/10.3389/fpsyg.2023.1221003 PMID: 37744611; PMCID: PMC10514504.

Ho, E. W., Strohmeier-Breuning, S., Rossanese, M., Charron, D., Pennise, D., & Graham, J. P. (2021). Diverse health, gender and economic impacts from domestic transport of water and solid fuel: A systematic review. *International Journal of Environmental Research and Public Health, 18*(19), 10355. https://doi.org/10.3390/ijerph181910355. PMID: 34639655; PMCID: PMC8507830.

Huyer, S., & Westholm, G. (2001). *Gender and climate change: A training manual.* International Union for Conservation of Nature (IUCN).

International Renewable Energy Agency. (2019). Renewable energy: A gender perspective. IRENA.

International Monetary Fund. (2020). *Jamaica and the IMF.* https://www.imf.org/en/Countries/JAMIMF

Jamaica Information Service. (2019). *Energy news.* https://jis.gov.jm/news/?category=energy

Jayaweera, S. A. A., et al. (1989). The effect of particle size on the combustion of Weardale coal. *Fuel, 68*(12), 1561–1565.

Jessel, S., Sawyer, S., & Hernández, D. (2019). Energy, poverty, and health in climate change: A comprehensive review of an emerging literature. *Frontiers in Public Health, 7*, 357. https://doi.org/10.3389/fpubh.2019.00357

Jimenez, M. P., DeVille, N. V., Elliott, E. G., Schiff, J. E., Wilt, G. E., Hart, J. E., & James, P. (2021). Associations between nature exposure and health: A review of the evidence. *International Journal of Environmental Research and Public Health, 18*(9), 4790. https://doi.org/10.3390/ijerph18094790

Kaygusuz, K. (2011). Energy services and energy poverty for sustainable rural development. *Renewable and Sustainable Energy Reviews, 15*(2), 936–947.

Makan, A. (1995). Power for women and men: Towards a gendered approach to domestic energy policy and planning in South Africa. *Third World Planning Review, 17*(2), 183–198. https://doi.org/10.3828/twpr.17.2.y951502074p2w545

Martins, A., Madaleno, M., & Dias, M. F. (2021). Women vs men: Who performs better on energy literacy? *International Journal of Sustainable Energy Planning and Management, 32*, 37–46. https://doi.org/10.5278/ijsepm.6516

Ministry of Science, Energy and Technology (MSET). (2019). *Jamaica Energy Balance 2019.* https://www.mset.gov.jm/wp-content/uploads/2019/06/Jamaica-Energy-Balance-2019.pdf

Modi, V., McDade, S., Lallement, D., & Saghir, J. (2005). *Energy services for the Millennium Development Goals.* United Nations Development Programme, UN Millennium Project, samy and World Bank.

Munien, S., & Ahmed, F. (2012). A gendered perspective on energy poverty and livelihoods–Advancing the Millennium Development Goals in developing countries. *Agenda, 26*(1), 112–123. https://doi.org/10.1080/10130950.2012.665146

Oliveras, L., Peralta, A., Palència, L., Gotsens, M., López, M. J., Artazcoz, L., Borrell, C., & Marí-Dell'Olmo, M. (2020). Energy poverty and health: Trends in the European Union before and during the economic crisis, 2007–2016. *Health & Place, 66,* 102294. https://doi.org/10.1016/j.healthplace. 2020.102294

Pearce, D., & Standing, G. (2001). *Globalisation, growth and inequality: Demonstrating a 'poverty bias' in world trade.* United Nations Development Programme.

Pei, A. (2021, October 7). *5 environmental benefits of sustainable transportation | UCLA transportation.* 5 Environmental Benefits of Sustainable Transportation. https://transportation.ucla.edu/blog/5-environmental-benefits-sustainable-transportation

Reddy, A. K. N. (2000). Energy and social issues. In J. Goldemberg (Ed.), *World Energy Assessment: Energy and the Challenge of Sustainability* (pp. 39–60). United Nations Development Programme.

Reddy, A. K. N., & Reddy, B. S. (1994). Subsidies and sustainable development: Key issues. *Energy for Sustainable Development, 1*(1), 17–24.

Rengasamy, S., et al. (2001). *Thaan Vuzha Nilam Tharisu – The land without a farmer becomes barren: Policies that work for sustainable agriculture and rural livelihoods in Virudhunagar District, Tamil Nadu.* International Institute for Environment and Development (IIED).

Robinson, C. (2019). Energy poverty and gender in England: A spatial perspective. *Geoforum, 104,* 222–233. https://doi.org/10.1016/j.geoforum.2019. 05.001

Rodgers, Y. v. d. M. (2022). Time poverty: Conceptualization, gender differences, and policy implications. *Social Philosophy & Policy,* forthcoming.

Rose, D. (2024). *Wigton accelerating diversification: Shareholders to vote on name change as company eyes opportunities away from wind.* Jamaica Observer. https://www.jamaicaobserver.com/

Sangha, P. S., Thakur, M., Akhtar, Z., Ramani, S., & Gyamfi, R. S. (2020). The link between rheumatoid arthritis and dementia: A review. *Cureus, 12*(4), e7855. https://doi.org/10.7759/cureus.7855. PMID: 32489719; PMCID: PMC7255531.

United Nations Development Programme. (2017). *Breaking up with fossil fuels.* Retrieved May 11, 2025, from https://featured.undp.org/breaking-up-with-fossil-fuels/

Williams, G. A. (2006). *An evaluation of the low-income housing sector in Jamaica.* (Master's thesis). Georgia Institute of Technology.

Winkler, H., et al. (2011). Access and affordability of electricity in developing countries. *World Development, 39*(6), 1037–1050.

World Bank. (1996). *Rural energy and development: Improving energy supplies for two billion people*. World Bank Development in Practice.

Xiao, Y., Wu, H., Wang, G., & Wang, S. (2021). The relationship between energy poverty and individual development: Exploring the serial mediating effects of learning behavior and health condition. *International Journal of Environmental Research and Public Health*, *18*(16), 8888. https://doi.org/10.3390/ijerph18168888. PMID: 34444636; PMCID: PMC8393606.

CHAPTER 2

Conceptual Framework

Abstract This chapter highlights the conceptual framework used to explore the role of women in relation to energy within their communities. Various approaches were identified and these include feminist political ecology which integrates feminist theory, goals, and practices with political ecology, an analytical framework that views ecological issues through the lens of political economy (and vice versa). This was important as it created a context for understanding the view point of gender and energy in these communities. Another approach is energy justice. This was used to showcase injustice and inequality in the energy industry using a multi-dimensional, human-centred theoretical approach, also helping us understand the planning and execution of energy systems. Other approaches also included the gender and development theory, this also looks at how people come to identify certain gender and how social norms and expectations shape their gendered roles and behaviours especially with regard to the use of energy. The social reproduction theory, technology adoption, and diffusion theory look at the current context of gender, it helps to understand how different gender groups affect and embrace technology. The participatory approach also spoke to diverse groups of people, while recognizing and addressing gender dynamics, in decision-making processes, development initiatives, and programmes and the ecofeminism

© The Author(s), under exclusive license to Springer Nature
Switzerland AG 2025
S. Walters, *Energy Poverty Among Women in Jamaica's Low-Income Communities*, https://doi.org/10.1007/978-3-031-89079-6_2

approach was investigated as it looks at feminism and political ecology that examines the relationships between humans and the natural world through the lens of gender.

Keywords Social reproduction theory • Technology adoption • Feminism and political ecology and diffusion theory

This book employs several conceptual frameworks to further examine the role of women in relation to energy within their communities. Critical feminist analysis argues that the liberal effort to merge a "gender-friendly" approach to poverty reduction with a commitment to neoliberal structural adjustment is ultimately restrictive. Developing countries face significant challenges, such as providing reliable, affordable, and modern energy services to facilitate economic development and poverty eradication, as well as enhancing the ability of the poor to adapt to changing energy service conditions despite limited purchasing power. A gendered analysis of energy poverty emphasizes the underlying gender dynamics and energy services, rather than focusing solely on women and energy.

The livelihoods framework aims to explore the connection between gender and energy services. This approach looks at the economic benefits of energy and how these services enhance people's livelihoods. Energy poverty is viewed as a developmental challenge rather than just an issue within the energy sector. The role of the energy sector in poverty reduction is to supply essential services (such as lighting, heating, and refrigeration) that can facilitate income generation. The availability of energy services can create more income-generating opportunities, potentially reducing households' dependence solely on agriculture for survival and improving the sustainability of their livelihoods.

Creating social and political networks rooted in the community is crucial in this situation, particularly for women who want to take use of credit and other resources. The paradigm emphasizes a people-centred approach and gives priority to the problems of the poor over the energy resources, buildings, or services they may consume. With the goal of achieving results that lessen poverty, it advocates entitlements to resources that support certain livelihoods. The framework emphasizes three main components: stakeholder differences, livelihood strategies, and changes in livelihoods as a result of access to energy services. Achieving the SDGs requires expanding access to energy services.

Since women and girls are frequently given household chores because of the gender division of labour that is common in many traditional patriarchal countries, addressing the gender gap in education is directly related to livelihood arrangements. Women are disproportionately affected by the hard and rigid work of gathering traditional fuels, which prevents them from achieving equal access to education, reduces their potential for generating an income, and keeps them from being able to overcome poverty. Girls and women spend a lot of time obtaining traditional fuels, which affects both their academic performance and school enrolment.

Access to energy is essential for advancing education at all levels for girls and women. Enhanced lighting extends daily productivity hours, allowing women and girls to engage more in adult education and dedicate additional time to reading and learning. In developing countries, it is crucial to support education for women and girls in fields like science, engineering, and technology, as well as to improve access to information through media such as radio, television, and the internet. Energy access programmes should particularly focus on women to boost their participation in energy decision-making processes. Reliable, affordable, and safe energy services are vital for fostering rural enterprises, enabling women to start small businesses like cooking for sale, sewing, and crafting.

Possibilities for earning revenue from new energy sources encourage joint and co-ownership partnerships, such as women's communal sewing and craft groups, and enhance income-generating activities, which in turn builds social networks and jobs. Furthermore, opportunities for altering gender labour roles can enable women to gain more control over household decision-making and address biases in the division of labour. Improved lighting in the home enhances women's literacy and educational attainment while also lengthening their working hours for income-generating activities ("Transforming the Future of Work for Gender Equality Initiative," n.d.).

FEMINIST POLITICAL ECOLOGY

Feminist political ecology is a specialized field that integrates feminist theory, goals, and practices with political ecology, an analytical framework that views ecological issues through the lens of political economy (and vice versa). Scholars in feminist political ecology argue that gender, alongside class, race, and other relevant factors, is a critical element in shaping access to, control over, and understanding of natural resources. According to

Clemente (2015), research in this area reveals how social identities are formed through interactions with nature and daily material practices.

Harcourt and Nelson (2015) discussed Feminist Political Ecology, describing it as an approach that redefines environmentalism, justice, and feminism. They view it as research and practice that extends political ecology to incorporate gendered power dynamics across various levels, from local and intra-household to intra-community and global scales. Feminist Political Ecology typically embraces feminist epistemology, methods, and values, focusing on research and practices that empower women and other marginalized groups while fostering social and ecological transformation.

Due to traditional caregiving and household responsibilities, women and girls experience the greatest amount of energy poverty in Jamaica, where single-parent households—which are predominantly led by women—represent the poor at a disproportionate rate. Therefore, any further growth of this sector will require the use of a gender lens. For women, having access to energy services has several advantages. For instance, having access to electricity enables the use of labour-saving devices and reduces the burning of wood, charcoal, and agricultural leftovers, all of which contribute to increased health and safety as well as improved household efficiency. The ease of access to electricity affects home-based businesses, many of which are owned and operated by women who market domestic services like cooking and sewing (UNDP, Engender, 2021).

High energy costs in the region disproportionately impact households with the lowest incomes. These families are more likely to have larger household sizes, poorer housing quality, and female heads of household. The resulting heavy energy burden can force them to make tough choices between housing, energy, food, education, and health. To address this issue, government intervention is necessary. Governments should consider providing targeted financial assistance with energy-saving incentives to protect vulnerable populations, particularly low-income single-parent households led by women with high dependency ratios (Brown et al., 2020).

Energy Justice

Building on the principles of environmental justice, energy justice encompasses the concepts of equity, affordability, accessibility, and participation within the energy system and energy transition, regardless of race, nationality, income, or geographic location. Energy is central to nearly every aspect of our lives, and energy policy is responsible for how energy is produced, delivered, and used globally, whether at the community, organizational, or governmental level. This is not without challenges (What is Energy Justice, 2021). The goal of energy justice is to alleviate injustice and inequality in the energy industry using a multidimensional, human-centred theoretical approach (Caribbean Development Bank, 2018). It accomplishes this by figuring out who ought to be involved in the planning and execution of energy systems, comprehending their effects, and figuring out who these systems influence. By establishing fairness in social, economic, and political involvement, the energy system will eventually become more moral.

The Jamaican government has shown a strong commitment to gender-responsive climate action through the creation of the Gender and Climate Change Strategy and Action Plan (GCCSAP). This plan is designed to guide the implementation of their commitment. One significant barrier to energy justice in Jamaica is the recognition that women's unpaid care responsibilities can increase their vulnerability to energy injustice and limit their ability to engage in policy discussions aimed at achieving energy equity solutions. Tasks such as household duties and caring for children and elderly family members consume a significant amount of time (PIOJ & STATIN, 2018), and this needs to be considered in the design and implementation of actions. Additionally, men outnumber women in the management and ownership of energy-service-related firms, largely due to the persistence of gender stereotypes.

The disciplines and careers that are promoted in the educational system are where bias first manifests itself. But increasing the number of women employed in the field won't guarantee that gender-related concerns are adequately handled. In order to find a solution, the government must first acknowledge that there is a need to promote a wide awareness of gender equality concerns, including how they relate to HRM and how they could impact both persons and businesses in the sector.

Gender and Development Theory

The study of gender development theory looks at how people come to identify as a certain gender and how social norms and expectations shape their gendered roles and behaviours. In Jamaica, gender development is influenced by a complex web of social, cultural, historical, and economic factors. Understanding the unique sociocultural context of Jamaica is essential for researching gender development in the nation. These concepts may be roughly categorized into three categories: cognitive, socialization, and biological. According to biological theories, biological differences between males and females account for psychological and behavioural gender differences (Miller, 2016).

Understanding gender development in Jamaica necessitates an integrative approach that takes into account how race, class, and sexuality connect with gender. In Jamaica, advocating for gender equality entails confronting both structural hurdles and cultural practices that may perpetuate inequality. The Jamaican structure hurdle consists mostly of patriarchal views, as though women have their matrifocal advantages, when it comes to the more powerful subsets like power and stability society chooses the male. Conversely, the Planning Institute of Jamaica (2022) asserts that Jamaica has achieved notable strides in the areas of women's empowerment and gender equality. This endeavour has been facilitated by several legislative initiatives and government institution-building efforts. The goal of the National Policy for Gender Equality (NPGE) is to uphold the gender equality concept.

It provides the foundation for a thorough and coordinated approach to integrating gender into all facets of national life. The NPGE emphasizes the importance of gender mainstreaming within Jamaica's Ministries, Departments, and Agencies (MDAs). Following the NPGE's guidelines, Jamaica has created and implemented its inaugural National Strategic Action Plan to combat gender-based violence, established partnerships and collaborations to gather and analyse gender-disaggregated data, enhanced advocacy for equity and equality across various laws and policies, and set up an accountability mechanism through the Gender Advisory Council.

The Vision 2030 Jamaica—National Development Plan 2009 Gender Sector Plan and the National Policy for Gender Equality (NPGE) 2011 provide the foundation for non-discrimination and the protection of all citizens' rights. Since 2018, the Government of Jamaica (GOJ) has been working to implement and strengthen the legislative and regulatory framework to combat gender discrimination. To ensure equality, non-discrimination under the law, and access to justice, various laws are being reviewed in accordance with the NPGE. These include the Sexual Offences Act (2009), the Offences Against the Person Act (1865, amended 2014), the Domestic Violence Act (1996), and the Child Care and Protection Act

(2004). Additionally, the Sexual Harassment (Protection and Prevention) Act of 2021 has been approved and passed. According to the Planning Institute of Jamaica (2022), there has been progress over the last five years in improving gender equality, empowering women and girls, and reducing discrimination, particularly in areas such as education and social security.

SOCIAL REPRODUCTION THEORY

Brenner (1989) argued that gender relations and social reproduction are both shaped by and shape micro historical processes. In feminist theory, social reproduction encompasses more than production in the Marxist sense. It involves a combination of the organization of production, social reproduction, gender perpetuation, and the continuation of class relations. Social reproduction includes activities such as caring for and socializing children and caring for the elderly or infirm. It also involves the organization of sexuality, biological reproduction, and the provision of essentials like food, clothing, and shelter. Most social reproduction occurs within the family unit. Changes in the distribution of social reproduction work are influenced by the family, market, community, and state.

According to the feminist perspective, social constructivists have looked at how society and culture have shaped even the most apparent gender disparities ("What is a feminist perspective? – An overview," 2020). According to them, a lot of the distinctions that are thought to be the cause of gender inequality should rather be seen as a byproduct of it (Feminist Perspectives on Reproduction and the Family, 2004). Conversely, different feminists want to honour and reaffirm the characteristics that have historically been connected to women. They contend that as long as there is voluntary participation and equal value placed on both male and female tasks, a sex-based division of labour is not intrinsically harmful.

Early social reproduction theorists emphasize the significance of household labour, recognizing and valuing the unpaid domestic work of women and its essential role in supporting waged labour under capitalism. A gendered perspective on the economy is a key element of contemporary social reproduction theory. Many caregiving tasks are categorized as domestic labour and thus assigned to women. Traditionally, tasks such as cleaning, cooking, and childrearing have been the responsibility of wives, mothers, and women in general, making their work both crucial and unpaid. As Finnamore (2023) points out, women also regenerate the workforce by giving birth. Social reproduction theory reveals their "invisible" labour, highlighting the intertwined rights of women and workers.

In the early twentieth century, Lenin (1870–1924) referred to women's status as "domestic slaves," a condition that persists globally today. The capitalist system perpetuates women's dependence on men as family breadwinners by designating domestic work as the "wife's" job and responsibility. For instance, in Jamaica, even an unemployed woman is expected to ensure the household runs smoothly, meals are prepared, children are cared for, and the breadwinner's needs are met. If she fails in these duties, the male breadwinner often asserts his power and dominance. One important criticism with the idea is its failure to address one issue. The Social Reproduction Theory is unduly focused on class conflict, ignoring the major influence of other types of exploitation and discrimination that are best understood through intersectionality.

Technology Adoption and Diffusion Theory

When Technology Adoption and Diffusion Theory is applied to the context of gender, it helps to understand how different gender groups affect and embrace technology. The theory's framework may be expanded to examine how technology adoption interacts with gender dynamics. Gender disparities in access to information and knowledge of new technologies may emerge. Women may encounter barriers to acquiring information about progress, especially in specific geographical or socioeconomic conditions. Gender economic differences may influence views of the relative benefits of adopting specific technology. Financial barriers may impede women's ability to embrace new technology.

Sociocultural norms and expectations can have an impact on how well an invention fits into established gender roles. Technologies that contradict or adhere to existing gender norms may experience various levels of acceptance. Women constitute 39% of the global workforce, but just 16% of the conventional energy industry (Energy and Gender, 2021). The numbers are significantly lower at the managerial level. Women face comparable obstacles in the energy sector as elsewhere in the business. Meanwhile, women suffer disproportionately from a lack of access to electricity or clean cooking fuels, which limits their career options, exposes them to health hazards, and forces them to scavenge for wood or other combustible materials.

According to previous research (Energy and Gender, 2021), there are significantly fewer women working in the energy industry compared to men. The gender disparity in this sector is more than twice as large as that in non-energy sectors. Additionally, female employees earn nearly 20% less than their male counterparts, with this pay gap being slightly wider than in non-energy businesses. Even when other factors are considered, the salary disparity remains nearly unchanged, indicating that the gap is not due to differences in skill levels between genders within companies.

According to the International Energy Agency (2022), males have historically dominated the energy sector, and its workforce is not reflective of the entire population or workforce. According to 2018 statistics from 29 countries (including 22 IEA members), 76% fewer women than males work in the energy industry, a significant difference from the 8% imbalance observed in the overall workforce. Women face comparable obstacles in the energy sector as elsewhere in the business. A proposal should be to look at strong and relevant policy options that would assist to close this gap, such as a gender quota system that may be implemented as a mandate in certain areas.

Participatory Approaches

A participatory approach in the context of gender refers to involving diverse groups of people, with a specific emphasis on recognizing and addressing gender dynamics, in decision-making processes, development initiatives, and programmes. This approach recognizes the importance of actively engaging both men and women, acknowledging their unique perspectives, experiences, and needs. The goal is to promote gender equality, empower marginalized groups, and create more inclusive and responsive outcomes. Participatory approaches in gender take into account the voices and perspectives of both men and women, as well as other gender identities. It aims to include individuals from different socioeconomic backgrounds, ethnicities, and abilities to ensure a diverse range of experiences is considered.

The strategy aims to empower women and other marginalized genders by allowing them to actively participate in decision-making processes. This empowerment entails acknowledging and appreciating their knowledge, abilities, and agency. Participatory gender projects' findings and recommendations are frequently used for lobbying and policy change. These initiatives can help to create more inclusive and gender-sensitive policies and programmes by actively involving affected groups. A participatory strategy with an emphasis on women in the energy sector entails actively including women in decision-making processes, project planning, implementation, and policy formation connected to energy projects. This strategy highlights women's particular roles, problems, and contributions in the energy sector, with the goal of promoting gender equality, empowering women, and improving the overall sustainability and efficacy of energy projects.

According to the International Energy Agency (2022), women incur a substantial cost as a result of limited access to power and clean cooking fuels. They are frequently entrusted with harvesting firewood or other polluting fuels, which requires a significant amount of time and work. Household air pollution, primarily from cooking smoke, causes roughly 2.5 million premature deaths each year, with women and children being the most impacted. In underdeveloped nations, where women are frequently employed in informal industries such as garment production or food preparation, a lack of electricity significantly limits their professional options.

The Equality in Energy Transitions initiative (formerly known as C3E International) was established in 2010 as part of the Clean Energy Ministerial (CEM) effort to promote gender equality and diversity in renewable energy transitions. In 2017, the initiative's activities were restructured as an IEA Technology Collaboration Program (TCP). This programme is designed to focus on gender inclusivity and address the societal gap between male and female stereotypes through a participatory approach.

Ecofeminism

Ecofeminism is a branch of feminism and political ecology that examines the relationships between humans and the natural world through the lens of gender (Bove, 2021). The term was introduced by French writer "Françoise d'Eaubonne" in her 1974 book titled "Le Féminisme ou la Mort." Ecofeminist theory offers a feminist perspective on green politics, advocating for a just and cooperative society without any dominant group. The current capitalist development model, driven by technology and economics, relentlessly promotes competition and the pursuit of unchecked wealth, reflecting a historic desire for patriarchal power. This model not only disadvantages various groups, including women, but is also unsustainable in the long run.

Ecofeminists see patriarchy as responsible for gender oppression, the plight of the poor, and the marginalization of indigenous people, as well as for production and consumption systems that treat nature as a commodity to be exploited and discarded (Buckingham, 2015). They argue that male dominance leads society towards greater destruction, as egotistical behaviour among men results in conflicts and coups that ultimately harm the environment. According to ecofeminists, just as women are oppressed, so too is nature, reflecting a similar pattern of exploitation. The assertion of masculine control perpetuates distress for both women and the environment.

Buckingham (2015) highlighted the work of philosophers and historians like Vandana Shiva and Carolyn Merchant, who have explored the global impact of patriarchal, colonial, and modernist forces—such as development and science—on women and nature. Their research reveals that both development and science are dominant social systems deeply intertwined with patriarchy and colonialism. Men in these systems work together to facilitate the ongoing extraction of resources and knowledge from the Global South to the North, while imposing "masculine" scientific knowledge in the South that marginalizes indigenous and women's ecological and scientific perspectives.

Ecofeminism includes various perspectives on how to engage with and advocate for the environment, but all ecofeminists agree on the essential connection between a healthy environment and the well-being of women and children. Ecofeminists see patriarchy as responsible for the oppression of women, marginalized communities, and indigenous peoples, as well as for production and consumption systems that treat nature as a mere commodity to be exploited and discarded. Buckingham (2015) noted that Sandra Harding and other feminist philosophers of science have argued that science and technology have significantly contributed to global patriarchal dominance. The supposed neutrality and objectivity of the scientific method have given science and its technological advancements an aura of certainty and inevitability. Science has largely been controlled by and has benefitted the wealthy and powerful, with men typically being the gatekeepers of this science and wealth generation.

Energy Democracy

Energy Democracy refers to a transition from a centralized, corporate-driven fossil fuel economy to one that is community-managed, grounded in environmental stewardship, supports local economies, and enhances the health and well-being of all people (Energy Democracy Climate Justice Alliance, 2023). Essentially, the concept advocates for the right and ability of communities and individuals to control and shape their own energy systems. It promotes a decentralized, participatory, and inclusive approach to energy decision-making and governance. Energy democracy fosters community involvement, local ownership, and equitable distribution of energy benefits and responsibilities. Analysing energy democracy through a gender perspective means integrating principles of gender equality and social justice into the design, implementation, and outcomes of energy systems.

Gender issues in energy democracy should include efforts to address historical gender disparities in energy resource ownership and control. Women's access to and ownership of renewable energy technology, as well as participation in decision-making bodies, contribute to the development of more equitable energy systems. With this access, projects supporting energy democracy would give opportunities for women's economic growth. This might include aiding female energy entrepreneurs, offering training and capacity-building programmes, and encouraging female participation in energy-related income-generating activities.

Recognizing and appreciating the gendered division of labour in energy-related tasks is critical. Women frequently take on prominent responsibilities in energy-related care work, such as cooking and childcare. Sustainable energy solutions should strive to lessen the time and effort that women put into such jobs. Addressing vulnerabilities would only promote progress among both genders and society. Women are disproportionately affected by energy-related vulnerabilities, such as energy poverty, in numerous circumstances. Energy democracy programmes should focus on eliminating these vulnerabilities and ensuring that women are not disproportionately affected by energy-related issues.

The United Nations Sustainability Hub states that access to energy is vital for ensuring good health, education, and economic development and is key to achieving all the Sustainable Development Goals, including SDG 5 on gender equality. Closing access gaps is essential for realizing gender equality. Women and girls face disproportionate health and safety risks due to their care work responsibilities, such as exposure to indoor air pollution from using dirty fuels and the burdens and dangers of travelling long distances to gather biomass. These responsibilities lead to considerable time poverty for women and girls, restricting their opportunities for income generation, education, and leisure. Our knowledge of how women function in society today is shaped by these many theoretical perspectives, particularly when examining more energy-focused domains. The many discussions that are offered in subsequent chapters were also informed by these notions.

References

Bove, T. (2021). *Ecofeminism: Where gender and climate change intersect*. Earth. Org. https://earth.org/ecofeminism/

Brenner, J. (1989). Gender and social reproduction: Historical perspectives. *Annual Review of Sociology, 15*, 381–404. JSTOR.

Brown, K., et al. (2020). *Toward a gender diverse workforce in the renewable energy transition*. https://www.researchgate.net/publication/306314469_Toward_a_gender_diverse_workforce_in_the_renewable_energy_transition

Buckingham, S. (2015). *Gender and the environment*. Routledge. https://www.routledge.com/Gender-and-the-Environment/Buckingham/p/book/9780415530446

Caribbean Development Bank. (2018). *Integrating gender equality into the energy sector*. https://www.caribank.org/sites/default/files/publicationresources/CDB8_INTEGRATING%20GENDER%20EQUALITY%20INTO%20THE%20ENERGY%20SECTOR_final.pdf

Clemente, J. (2015, January 22). End energy poverty and empower women. *Forbes*. https://www.forbes.com/sites/judeclemente/2015/01/22/alleviating-energy-poverty-and-empowering-females/

Energy Democracy Climate Justice Alliance. (2023, July 10). *Climate Justice Alliance*. https://climatejusticealliance.org/workgroup/energy-democracy/#:~:text=What%20is%20Energy%20Democracy%3F,well%2Dbeing%20for%20all%20peoples

Finnamore, E. (2023, January 21). *Social Reproduction Theory and women in society*. Rupture. https://rupture.ie/articles/social-reproduction-theory-and-women-in-society

Harcourt, W., & Nelson, I. L. (Eds.). (2015). *Practising feminist political ecologies: Moving beyond the "Green Economy"*. Zed Books. UN Women.

International Energy Agency (IEA). (2021). *Energy and gender*. https://www.iea.org/topics/energy-and-gender

International Energy Agency. (2022). https://www.iea.org/reports/renewables-2022

Miller, C. (2016). *A review of gender, social equity and low-carbon energy.* https://www.sciencedirect.com/science/article/pii/S2214629620303492

Planning Institute of Jamaica. (2022). Gender assessment study: Final report. https://www.pioj.gov.jm/product/gender-assessment-study-final-report/

Planning Institute of Jamaica (PIOJ) & Statistical Institute of Jamaica (STATIN). (2018). *The report on the Jamaica Survey of Establishments 2018.* https://www.pioj.gov.jm/product/the-report-on-the-jamaica-survey-of-establishments-2018-3/

Stanford Encyclopedia of Philosophy. (2004). *Feminist perspectives on reproduction and the family.* https://plato.stanford.edu/entries/feminism-family/

United Nations Development Programme (UNDP). (n.d.). *Transforming the future of work for gender equality initiative.* https://jobs.undp.org/cj_view_job.cfm?job_id=88905

United Nations Development Programme (UNDP). (2021). *EnGenDER Highlights.* https://www.undp.org/barbados/engender-highlights

University of Sussex. (2021). *What is energy justice?* https://study-online.sussex.ac.uk/news-and-events/what-isenergy-justice/

What is feminist political ecology (FPE)? - wego-ITN. (2020, May 19). WEGO. https://www.wegoitn.org/online-learning/what-is-feminist-political-ecology-fpe/

CHAPTER 3

The Impact of Energy Poverty on Gender

Abstract This chapter examines and explores the impact of energy poverty on gender. It goes further to look at the complex nature that vulnerable women are affected by their use and interpretation of the various forms of energy. This chapter examines the body of research on how energy poverty affects gender, with a focus on women. It starts by providing a global definition of energy poverty and its causes. The impact of energy poverty on women's health, education, and economic prospects is then examined in detail. Potential remedies to energy poverty and gender equity are also covered in this chapter. The chapter concludes by offering suggestions on how stakeholders and legislators can combat energy poverty and advance gender parity.

Globally, energy poverty affects millions of women, manifesting as inadequate access to essential energy services like electricity, clean cooking fuels, and heating. Women are more severely impacted by energy poverty because their gender roles often involve managing households and caregiving tasks. Additionally, lower incomes and reduced access to education further exacerbate their vulnerability to the adverse effects of energy poverty.

Keywords Energy poverty • Women health • Education and Economic Opportunities • Global

The Impact of Energy Poverty on Gender Particularly on Women in a Global Perspective

As discussed in Chap. 1, energy poverty is defined as the lack of access to sufficient and affordable energy services, which significantly impacts gender, particularly women. The effects of energy poverty on gender are complex, with women being especially vulnerable due to their gender-specific roles and responsibilities. Globally, energy poverty affects millions of women, manifesting as inadequate access to essential energy services like electricity, clean cooking fuels, and heating. Women are more severely impacted by energy poverty because their gender roles often involve managing households and caregiving tasks. Additionally, lower incomes and reduced access to education further exacerbate their vulnerability to the adverse effects of energy poverty.

Indrawati (2023) stated that energy poverty is driven by various factors, including income, geography, and policy. In low-income countries, energy poverty is often linked to poverty and lack of infrastructure. Middlemiss (2022) then added that in high-income countries, energy poverty is more likely to affect marginalized communities, such as indigenous populations and low-income households. It can be considered that geography also drives energy poverty, with rural populations more likely to experience energy poverty than urban populations. The impact of energy poverty on gender is multi-faceted, affecting women's health, education, and economic opportunities.

This chapter examines the body of research on how energy poverty affects gender, with a focus on women. It starts by providing a global definition of energy poverty and its causes. The impact of energy poverty on women's health, education, and economic prospects is then examined in detail. Potential remedies to energy poverty and gender equity are also covered in this chapter. The chapter concludes by offering suggestions on how stakeholders and legislators can combat energy poverty and advance gender parity.

A Global Perspective of Energy Poverty

Millions of people worldwide are impacted by the complicated and multifaceted subject known as energy poverty. "A lack of access to modern energy services" is how the International Energy Agency (IEA) defines energy poverty (IEA, 2017, p. 10). Lack of access to clean cooking fuels, power, and heating are just a few ways that this deficiency might show up. Three factors contribute to energy poverty, according to the IEA: (1) lack of access, (2) affordability, and (3) reliability. When energy services, such as electricity or clean cooking fuels, are unavailable, it is referred to as lack of access. The ability of households to pay for energy services is referred to as affordability, whilst the availability of energy services is referred to as reliability.

The world still must make progress to achieve Sustainable Development Goal 7 (SDG 7), which calls for ensuring that everyone has access to modern, affordable, sustainable, and dependable energy by 2030. By 2030, everyone must have equitable and equal access to reliable, affordable, and advanced energy services, according to SDG 7. Furthermore, by 2030, it will considerably raise the share of renewable energy in the global energy mix. Furthermore, by 2030, increase international collaboration to double the rate of global energy efficiency growth. This will facilitate public access to clean energy research and technology, such as cleaner and more advanced fossil fuel technology, renewable energy, and energy efficiency.

Encourage investment in renewable energy technologies and energy infrastructure as well. Finally, by 2030, all developing countries should have access to contemporary, sustainable energy services, with a particular emphasis on the least developed, small island developing states, and landlocked developing countries in accordance with their specific assistance initiatives (United Nations, 2022).

The Sustainable Development Goals Report (2022) highlights that global access to energy rose from 83% in 2010 to 91% in 2020. However, 733 million people still lack electricity, and 2.4 billion continue to use harmful fuels for cooking, which negatively impacts health and the environment. Between 2018 and 2020, the average annual increase in electricity access was 0.5 percentage points, compared to 0.8 percentage points from 2010 to 2018. If current trends persist, only 92% of the global population will have electricity access by 2030, leaving 670 million people without power. Additionally, due to economic pressures from the COVID-19 pandemic, up to 90 million people in Africa and developing Asia might struggle to afford a full range of services in 2021.

According to the Sustainable Development Goals Report (2021), between 2010 and 2020, the share of people using clean cooking fuels and technologies grew from 57% to 69%. Despite this progress, in 2020, 4 billion people still depended on inefficient and polluting cooking methods. In 2019, the share of renewable energy in total final energy consumption rose by 1.6 percentage points compared to 2010. Global primary energy intensity, which measures energy efficiency, improved from 5.6 megajoules per US dollar in 2010 to 4.7 in 2019, reflecting an average annual improvement rate of 1.9%. To meet the energy efficiency target by 2030, the annual progress rate must increase to 3.2%.

GLOBAL FINANCE OF ENERGY POVERTY

In 2019, international public financial transfers for renewable energy to developing countries totalled $10.9 billion, marking a decrease of approximately 24% compared to 2018. Furthermore, the five-year moving average of these transfers fell for the first time since 2008, dropping from $17.5 billion for the period 2014–2018 to $16.6 billion for 2015–2020.

> … *For us (Jamaica) to have access to greater energy sources we need to recruit cash from other countries as a number of the people would like to look at other energy sources but lack the money to do so….* (Renewable Energy Systems Training (REST), 2022)

Concurrently, the perceived level of risk associated with lending money to several developing nations has increased dramatically, making it more challenging for those nations to secure debt financing for energy-related technologies and enhance energy accessibility. The ability of many developing nations to absorb shocks and make investments in recovery is greatly hampered by a lack of funds. In their report "Bridging the 'great finance divide' in developing countries," Spiegel and Schwank (2022) observe that, thanks to the assistance of their central banks, developed countries were able to finance significant budgetary response measures (equivalent to 18 percentage points of GDP) at extremely low interest rates in the wake of the COVID-19 pandemic. Developing countries faced more restrictions. The need to cut back on infrastructure and education, especially in the poorest countries, resulted in a protracted crisis.

Before the impact of the war in Ukraine was fully realized, forecasts indicated that by the end of 2023, one in five emerging economies would still not reach the per capita income levels of 2019. It was also anticipated that it would take at least two years for investment rates to return to pre-pandemic levels (Spiegel & Schwank, 2022). Spiegel and Schwank's report highlights that the slow recovery in investment is exacerbating significant gaps in funding for climate change and Sustainable Development Goals

(SDGs). Many countries are struggling to secure the necessary resources for these investments. By 2022, one in four middle-income countries faced a high risk of fiscal collapse, while three out of five of the world's poorest nations were nearing or already experiencing debt crises. The war in Ukraine has intensified the strain on fiscal and external balances of commodity importers, with rising energy and food costs adding to the pressure, and tighter global financial conditions heightening systemic crisis risks.

In developing countries, concerns about debt sustainability often arise at relatively low levels of debt, leading to higher risk premiums. This high borrowing cost hampers essential investments, even in countries with manageable debt. However, the outlook for renewables and energy efficiency is positive. The rise in prices in 2021 and the focus of recovery plans in major economies on renewables and efficiency have bolstered their prospects. Despite recent price spikes and the uncertainties introduced by the Ukraine crisis, which have intensified pressure on net importers to minimize their exposure, renewables, efficiency, and electrification are expected to play crucial roles in policy responses to global disruptions. For the energy-related Sustainable Development Goals (SDGs) to be met, these responses need to be robust and extend beyond advanced economies (International Energy Agency, 2022).

Advancing SDG 7 relies on ongoing government backing for clean energy and energy access investments. As policymakers plan their strategies, they should consider that an ambitious energy transition aimed at achieving SDG 7 can also support other social and economic objectives. A well-structured energy transition can drive sustained economic growth, generate employment opportunities, and enhance overall welfare through comprehensive policies.

Innovative Technologies Globally

Emerging policies and technologies continue to advance the energy sector, but the COVID-19 pandemic has significantly impeded progress towards universal energy access. With current and planned policies, the world is unlikely to achieve SDG 7, and some targets have moved further out of reach. At the current pace, 670 million people are projected to lack electricity by 2030, 10 million more than previously estimated (International Energy Agency, 2022). The situation is further worsened by Russia's invasion of Ukraine, which is expected to slow progress on

SDG 7 targets even more. The access gap has widened regionally, with the 20 countries with the lowest electricity access housing 76% of the global population. Nearly 90 million people in Asia and Africa who previously had electricity are now unable to meet their basic energy needs (United Nations Department of Economic and Social Affairs, 2023).

Impact of Energy Poverty on Women Globally

The effects of energy poverty on gender, especially on women, are complex and significant. Women are disproportionately impacted by energy poverty due to their roles in household management and care work, which rely heavily on access to energy services. Additionally, women often have lower incomes and limited educational opportunities, exacerbating their vulnerability to energy poverty (United Nations, 2022). In Europe, energy poverty is a pressing issue as households face rising energy costs. News European Parliament reports that single mothers and other single women are more likely to struggle with energy bills compared to single men, largely due to declining average wages and an increase in low-paying, part-time, or precarious jobs.

In the EU, the gender pay gap remained at 13% in 2020 and had barely altered over the previous ten years. It indicates that women make 13% less per hour on average than males. The cost-of-living problem is detrimental to women's fundamental rights, economic and social inclusion, and health. Also, it makes it more difficult for women to leave an abusive spouse with whom they are financially dependent when they don't have a job or have a poor income. Indian economist and Nobel laureate Amartya Sen (2001) asserts that a lack of access to energy deprives individuals of essential needs like heating, lighting, and cooking fuel, as well as hindering their overall development. India remains far from achieving Sustainable Development Goal 7, which aims to "Ensure access to affordable, reliable, sustainable, and modern energy for all."

With a population of approximately 1.4 billion people, around 780 million in India still lack access to modern energy sources and rely on traditional methods such as biomass for cooking (Worldometer, 2023). Despite advances in household electrification through initiatives like the Pradhan Mantri Ujjwala Yojana (PMUY), there are still about 239 million people in India without access to electricity.

According to India's 2011 Census, about 87% of the rural population continues to use solid fuels for cooking, and it is projected that by 2030,

580 million people in the country will still lack access to clean cooking fuels. Energy poverty has a particularly severe impact on women due to societal and cultural expectations that place the primary responsibility for acquiring food and energy on them. Women, who represent 70% of the 1.3 billion people living in poverty, face additional barriers due to limited access to technology and resources. These constraints contribute to women's time poverty, poor health, and increased labour, putting them at a disadvantage in terms of economic and social development.

Not a lot of women are represented in climate change and the green economy. We have 1 or 2 women who participate in renewable energy from the academic and the finance perspective ...... (Representative from Bureau of Gender Affairs, 2022)

Women are significantly underrepresented in key sectors of the green economy, such as renewable energy, manufacturing, construction, and public transportation. In India, rural women, who have extensive traditional knowledge and a deep understanding of local needs, could play a crucial role in advancing the country's green economy transition. India is responsible for approximately 25% of the global 4.3 million premature deaths annually due to Household Air Pollution (HAP). In the country, 400 million people, predominantly women (90%), rely on solid biomass for cooking, exposing them to serious health risks like respiratory and pulmonary diseases and conditions such as blurred vision. Globally, around 3 billion people lack access to improved cooking technologies.

India's slow shift to clean and modern energy is partly due to a lack of awareness about the gender aspects of energy poverty. The impact of relying on traditional fuels is particularly severe for women. In rural India, women spend between five and eight hours daily on cooking-related tasks, with collecting fuelwood taking up about 20% of this time. This heavy workload adversely affects their health, exacerbated by poor nutrition and the physical demands of transporting 40 kg of wood over 2.5 kilometres twice a week. Cooking under poorly lit conditions with inefficient biomass stoves that contribute to indoor air pollution further increases their risk of anaemia, respiratory diseases, and complications during pregnancy and childbirth (Laxmi et al., 2003).

Similarly, in Jamaica, the issue of poor nutrition and the strenuous physical demands on women also pose significant health challenges. Many rural Jamaican women face similar hardships, such as carrying heavy loads of water or agricultural produce and cooking with inefficient stoves that emit harmful smoke. These conditions contribute to respiratory illnesses and other health problems, particularly affecting pregnant women and young children. A study by the Pan American Health Organization highlights that indoor air pollution from traditional cooking methods is a major health risk, leading to chronic respiratory diseases (PAHO, 2018). Moreover, the nutritional deficiencies prevalent in these communities increase the susceptibility to anaemia, impacting maternal and child health outcomes (Gordon-Strachan et al., 2014). Addressing these challenges in Jamaica requires integrated efforts to improve nutritional education, provide access to clean cooking technologies, and enhance rural infrastructure.

By implementing these interventions, it is possible to reduce the health burdens on rural women and improve overall community well-being. Addressing these issues requires multifaceted interventions, including improving nutritional status, reducing the physical burden through better infrastructure and technology, and providing access to cleaner cooking methods. These changes are vital for enhancing the health and well-being of these women, ultimately contributing to better maternal and child health outcomes thus eliminating the risks of prenatal mortality and postnatal complications (Laxmi et al., 2003). Addressing these issues requires multifaceted interventions, including improving nutritional status, reducing the physical burden through better infrastructure and technology, and providing access to cleaner cooking methods. These changes are vital for enhancing the health and well-being of these women, ultimately contributing to better maternal and child health outcomes.

For Indian women, energy poverty inevitably results in time poverty. It keeps them from working or participating in other activities that bring in money, from going to school, from learning new things, and from adjusting to and reducing the effects of climate change. The main reason a woman's family cannot switch from conventional to clean cooking fuel is because she does not have decision-making authority in the home. Because they provide for the family, the males have more influence over financial and other decisions. The question is, what are men willing to invest in? For example, when it comes to cooking fuel, they prioritize spending on traditional fuel rather than the clean alternative. Because the decision-makers don't understand or care about a woman's struggles with conventional cooking fuel, the family still relies on wood. Even people who are aware of the harmful health effects of traditional fuel might not prioritize spending their hard-earned money on a less-polluting alternative.

Climate change and its extreme weather events disrupt food supplies, natural resources, and traditional food sources. This makes it harder for people to find essential items like clean water and firewood, especially for women who often must travel farther to find them. Floods contaminate water supplies with harmful substances like arsenic, posing significant health risks, particularly for women and children responsible for ensuring safe drinking water. While technology can offer solutions, many rural women lack the resources, income, power, and land ownership to access these tools. This prevents them from using technologies like solar energy or clean water solutions, further limiting their ability to cope with climate change impacts.

About 60 million new employments will be created by the green economy in the next 20 years, with a large share of those positions being in technology and infrastructure. Investments in renewable energy, including hydro, geothermal, wind, and solar power, are thought to be able to produce 40% of these green jobs. Off-grid energy systems have enormous potential for enabling the switch from fossil fuels to clean, contemporary energy and for generating green jobs for women. In remote locations where grid electricity is not possible, off-grid solar energy (mini-grid, micro-grid, and stand-alone grid) can reach those places. In the long run, they are also more dependable and economical, and they can open the door for the switch to renewable energy sources and a decrease in carbon emissions. Off-grid solar energy can benefit rural households because they use less energy (International Labour Organization, 2018; International Renewable Energy Agency, 2019).

Around three-quarters of the 770 million people who live without electricity are in sub-Saharan Africa. Following six years of steady decline, data from the International Energy Agency indicates that COVID-19 is reversing this positive trend in Africa. Additionally, the rise in global poverty levels may have already made basic electricity services unaffordable for over 100 million former electricity users in Asia and Africa. These data are despite recent improvements.

Although it is a worldwide issue, women are disproportionately affected by energy poverty since they are the main consumers and providers of energy in households, and it is particularly acute in developing nations. According to estimates, up to 30% of households in some OECD nations lack access to energy, which disproportionately puts women and girls at risk for health issues and restricts their access to economic and educational possibilities (OECD, 2018).

Women and girls in underdeveloped nations face obstacles to their economic prospects and general well-being due to a lack of access to energy. A large amount of the day is spent by women and girls in rural regions gathering fuelwood, which contributes to poverty and inequality as well as lost possibilities for education and paid work (OECD, 2018). Much of Africa is affected by this, with Sierra Leone, Niger, and Cameroon having particularly high rates. Up to 20 hours a week are spent by women in Bangladesh, Nepal, and India gathering biomass fuel for heating and cooking.

Girls' access to education is hampered by the time they spend gathering biomass fuel. Household electrification increases female school attendance and employment opportunities in the long run. Brazilian studies show that females who grow up in rural regions with access to electricity have a 59% higher chance of finishing elementary education by the age of 18. Additionally, evidence shows that more access to electricity enhanced men's and women's job chances, with women benefitting most from the reduction of time spent on housework due to the usage of electric equipment (World Bank, 2015; Energia, 2017).

The effects of energy poverty on educational outcomes are detrimental across generations. It is often known that a mother's level of education and her children's health are related. Lower educated mothers have lower immunization rates and greater incidence of baby stunting. According to a study conducted in 175 countries between 1970 and 2009, half of the drops in child mortality were attributable to better women's education. A lack of educational opportunities deters future generations from going to school, which feeds the cycle (Smith & Haddad, 2015; World Bank, 2010).

Women are concerned about how access to safe energy might impact that individual as they are often concerned about the impact it has on their health and their family...... (Representative from the Gender Coalition, 2022)

Women and girls' health and well-being are directly impacted by energy poverty in a major way. The repercussions of air pollution disproportionately affect people in low- and middle-income countries as well as lower-income groups in higher-income ones ("Energy poverty disproportionately affects women and girls," n.d.). This is especially felt by women and girls, who are the world's main producers and consumers of domestic energy.

Air pollution puts pregnant women at higher risk. Recent data suggests that tiny particles from air pollution can enter the placenta and expose foetuses, which has been related to detrimental effects on fertility, pregnancy, and babies.

Dangerous work associated with energy resource access is linked to gender-based violence (GBV). Meaning, traditional gender roles in many societies require males to be the main providers of income, with women often taking on caregiving responsibilities or working in lower-paying occupations. Men who work in hazardous jobs for energy resources may feel stressed out about their jobs' instability or the risks they face on the job. Sometimes, this tension shows out as violence or hostility against women. Moreover, because they are a minority in the workforce, women who work in these fields may experience harassment and discrimination from their male co-workers. This may result in a culture that normalizes or ignores GBV. Women who reside in areas where the exploitation of energy resources is a major industry frequently face financial vulnerability. Because males predominate in these industries' high-paying occupations, women may have less access to money or influence over home decisions.

Women who are economically dependent may be more vulnerable to gender-based violence because they may feel pressured to put up with abusive relationships out of concern for their financial security ("Implications of gender roles in natural resource governance in Latin America and the Caribbean," 2021). Women and children are the primary victims of indoor pollution caused by inefficient cooking stoves, widely used in the Global South. Because women spend more time at home than men, they are more vulnerable to polluting fuels and insufficient heating, especially if they do not have access to modern cooking facilities ("Household air Pollution," 2021). The World Health Organization (WHO) estimates that because indoor air pollution raises the risk of stroke, pneumonia, lung disease, cancer, asthma, and other illnesses, it kills over 4 million people annually, mostly women and children ("Household and Air pollution," 2023).

More than 25% of the world's population has limited access to clean, efficient lighting energy and depends on biomass for cooking and warmth. There has been much written on the detrimental impacts of traditional biomass use—such as burning wood, manure, and agricultural residues—on ecosystems, agriculture, and public health. Kerosene lamps are common for lighting in most poor countries, and kerosene is regularly marketed as a cleaner cooking fuel substitute for solid fuels like biomass and coal ("Billions of people will lack access to safe water, sanitation and hygiene in 2030 unless progress quadruples – warn WHO, UNICEF," 2021).

Due to disparities in cultural expectations regarding men's and women's roles and duties in families, communities, and the means of earning a livelihood, men and women are affected by natural catastrophes and climate change differently.

> ... Me need to have access to cheap electricity. I am not really concerned about climate change. Is plenty money for bills...... (Focus Group Representative, 2022)

Women are more susceptible to many natural catastrophes and the consequences of climate change because they typically have lower incomes, fewer access points to credit, less decision-making authority, and less control over resources. Disasters and climate change often exacerbate gender disparities already present between men and women; thus, institutions must take gender variations into consideration when developing policies and providing services. In order to guarantee that men and boys, as well as women and girls, have equal access to disaster risk resilience, climate change, and environmental solutions, gendered disparities must be identified and addressed in climate change and disaster risk preparation and response initiatives (Engender, 2022).

WOMEN'S HEALTH AND ITS IMPACT BY ENERGY POVERTY

Women's health is significantly impacted by energy poverty. Women are forced to rely on traditional biomass fuels like wood, charcoal, and animal dung since they do not have access to clean cooking fuels like liquefied petroleum gas (LPG) or electricity. These fuels emit dangerous pollutants including particulate matter and carbon monoxide, which can lead to respiratory issues as well as other health issues. Due to their increased time spent in the home, women and children are more susceptible to the negative health effects of indoor air pollution.

The World Health Organization (WHO) estimates that indoor air pollution causes 4.3 million fatalities a year, the majority of which are caused by women and children (WHO, 2018). The main cause of indoor air pollution is the use of conventional biomass fuels for heating and cooking. Cooking with traditional biomass fuels puts women at risk for respiratory conditions like pneumonia and chronic bronchitis, as well as other ailments like headaches and irritated eyes.

Having access to energy is important for women especially with providing for myself and my family. It is also key during their menstruation as women need the resources to be better able to guard themselves during that time of the month.
(Focus Group representative, 2022)

Women's reproductive health is impacted by energy poverty as well. It can be challenging for women to practise good hygiene during their periods when they lack access to electricity and clean water, which can result in infections and other health issues. Furthermore, especially in rural regions, women may find it more difficult to get healthcare services if they do not have access to electricity. The capacity of healthcare facilities to deliver quality care can also be impacted by a lack of energy, especially in emergency situations.

THE ROLE OF ENERGY POVERTY AND EDUCATION

My children need electricity to study. I am from "Shodely", in Manchester and we always have problem with light and water, and it affect my children ....
(Focus Group representative, 2022)

Energy poverty also has a significant impact on women's education. The lack of access to electricity and other energy services can make it difficult for girls to attend school, particularly in rural areas. Girls may have to spend several hours each day collecting firewood or water, reducing the time they must study. In addition, the lack of lighting can make it difficult for girls to study at night.

Energy poverty is one of the causes contributing to the 130 million girls who are not attending school globally, according to the United Nations Educational, Scientific, and Cultural Organization (UNESCO, 2019). It might be challenging to deliver a quality education in some nations where schools are required to have access to energy. It may also be challenging for schools to offer computer-based instruction, which is becoming more and more crucial in the modern world, if there is no access to electricity.

Economic Opportunities and Energy Poverty

Women's economic chances are significantly impacted by energy poverty as well ("Women, Energy, and Economic Empowerment," 2018). Women frequently handle caregiving and household administration, which necessitates having access to energy services. Women may find it challenging to seek chances for education and training or to participate in activities that generate cash due to a lack of energy services. According to the International Labour Organization (ILO), women are more likely than men to work in the informal sector, where access to energy services is limited (ILO, 2019).

> *I have been a helper for almost 15 years that is what I use to pay my bills and to send my children to school lol I don't have any insurance. miss* (Focus group representative, 2022)

Women in the informal sector may work as street vendors, domestic workers, or in other low-paying jobs. These jobs often need to provide benefits such as sick leave, health insurance, or retirement savings, making it difficult for women to save money or invest in their future. Women are more likely than men to work in the unorganized sector, where access to energy services is constrained, according to the International Labour Organization (ILO) (Statistics on women, ILOSTAT, 2019). Women who work in the unorganized sector may be employed as housekeepers, street sellers, or in other low-wage positions. For women to save money or make investments in their future, these positions frequently require benefits like paid time off, health insurance, or retirement savings. Furthermore, women are frequently in charge of time-consuming and physically taxing household tasks like cooking and cleaning.

How Do We Encourage Energy and Promote Gender Equity?

Gender inequality and energy poverty are interwoven issues that have a substantial impact on socioeconomic development, especially in emerging nations like Jamaica. In order to promote sustainable growth, raise living standards, and guarantee equal opportunity for all, it is imperative that these challenges be addressed. To wrap up this chapter, several strategies for reducing energy poverty and advancing gender parity in Jamaica are included below. These strategies highlight the significance of integrated methods that take gender dynamics and energy access into account.

Energy Sources in Jamaica

Jamaica predominantly secures its energy from a mix of imported fossil fuels, making the electricity cost very high. This dependency therefore results in a high financial consumption of electricity bills to support their energy use. However, while the country is geographically located with greater access to the sun and in some parishes access to the wind and water through rivers, there needs to be more utilisation of renewable energy especially by women who live in low-income households. This is also a result of several factors such as issues with the infrastructure, the cost, and irregularities regarding policies regarding renewable energy in Jamaica. Households that do benefit are seen to be a part of the high-income bracket within Jamaica (World Bank Group, 2019).

Some of the renewable energy utilized in Jamaica is based on the sun through the photovoltaic solar system, wind farms and Hydropower Plants which are generated through water from rivers. A key indication shared by Prime Minister Mr. Holness in Oct 2018 is that Jamaica has a 50% target of offering renewable energy by 2030 (JIS, 2018). However according to the Ministry of Science and Technology, in 2024, renewable energy contributes approximately 19% to Jamaica's energy mix. This contribution is linked to solar farms such as the Content Solar Plant located in Clarendon which provides a capacity of 20 MW and the Paradise Park Solar Farm which is also located in Westmoreland and also offers a capacity of 51 MW (Ministry of Science and Technology, 2024). Along with these energy farms local residents and commercial also benefit from solar plants they would have generated at home to alleviate their energy costs and encourage a reduction in their electricity bills which as stated several low-income families do not have the million that is needed to procure the solar units, batteries, chargers etc.

Wind energy farms include Wigton Wind Farm in Manchester that also offers a total capacity of 62.7 MW and Munroe Wind Farm in St. Elizabeth which offers 3 MW. These farms also supply power to the national grid and hydropower plants such as the Maggoty Hydroelectric Plant in St. Elizabeth, contributing to electricity generation. of 6 MW, Upper River, St. Ann, 5 MW. Lower River, St. Ann 3 MW. Rio Bueno located in

Trelawny 2.5 MW, and Rams Hornin St. Andrew has 0.4 MW capacity (Rose, 2024).

Some solar energy also offers a hybrid approach where they utilize wind or diesel to ensure a renewable energy source. These are often found in communities that are rural in sections of St. Elizabeth and St. Ann. They utilize these hybrids to offer power to areas without consistent sources of electricity.

Most Jamaicans utilise the sun unconventionally. They use it to dry their clothes. They use it to dry their vegetables even though they do not have access to solar technology ... (Interview with lecture, 2022)

Solar Energy: Expanding solar energy projects can provide reliable and sustainable electricity to remote communities. Initiatives like the installation of solar panels in schools, healthcare centres, and homes can significantly reduce energy poverty. Programmes that train women in solar technology installation, and maintenance can promote gender equity by providing them with new skills and employment opportunities.

Wind Energy: Jamaica's coastal regions offer substantial potential for wind energy. Developing wind farms can contribute to the national grid and create jobs. Involving women in the planning, construction, and operation of these projects ensures that they benefit from the economic opportunities created.

The Grid-Connected Energy System

Jamaica's energy sector is now experiencing substantial transition as the country strives for a more sustainable and renewable energy future. The energy landscape includes both grid-connected and off-grid alternatives, which are critical for addressing energy access and sustainability throughout the island. The grid-connected energy system in Jamaica serves as the backbone of the country's energy infrastructure, supplying power to the bulk of urban and suburban regions. The Jamaica Public Service Company (JPS) manages the national grid and has the monopoly on energy transmission and distribution.

The grid consists of approximately 14,000 kilometres of transmission and distribution lines, including 400 kilometres of 138 kilovolt (kV) lines, over 800 kilometres of 69 kV lines, 12 138/69 kV interbud transformers, and 54 substation transformers ("Over J$600M Invested in Upgrading

Grid Technology since 2020," 2023). According to Powell (2016), "the grid's energy mix has traditionally been dominated by fossil fuels, primarily oil, making the system expensive and vulnerable to price instability caused by swings in global oil prices." However, Jamaica has made tremendous progress in diversifying its energy sources in recent years.

Jamaica produced its first comprehensive energy plan in 2009, including objectives for renewable energy, energy efficiency, and greenhouse gas emissions. According to the Office of the Prime Minister (2018), "The plan's renewable energy targets include expanding the usage of renewable energy in the entire energy mix to 20% by 2030, boosting renewable energy's share of electricity generation to 30% by 2030, and lowering energy intensity by more than 50% between 2015 and 2030." Renewable energy sources, especially solar and wind power, have increasingly been integrated into the grid-connected energy system. Initiatives such as the Wigton Windfarm and Paradise Park Solar Farm represent significant progress in decreasing the nation's reliance on imported oil and in reducing greenhouse gas emissions.

The grid-connected system nevertheless confronts a number of difficulties in spite of these developments. Despite being less frequent, power outages are still a problem in some areas because of deteriorating infrastructure and increased susceptibility to natural disasters. More comprehensive grid upgrading is also required to handle the growing proportion of sporadic renewable energy sources, such as solar and wind. Batteries and improved smart grid technologies are essential for controlling the unpredictable nature of renewable energy sources and guaranteeing a steady, dependable supply.

Off-Grid Power Options

Off-grid renewable energy could be crucial to Jamaica's energy revolution. Instead of extending the national grid, solutions can be put into place more quickly and with less capital expenditure. Particularly in regions with little or no grid connectivity (St. Thomas and Hanover, for example), solar power may supply reasonably priced electricity and is ideally adapted to Jamaica's sunny climate. Apart from helping individual houses, off-grid solutions can also help community-level services like small businesses, clinics, and schools, which will boost the local economy.

However, there are drawbacks to off-grid alternatives as well, including the high initial costs of setup and upkeep and the requirement for robust local capacity to support these systems. According to Munsell (2017), "the average cost of installing a home solar system in the Caribbean is $3.85 per watt, with significant price variations across islands, ranging from $1.50 per watt in Antigua to $8.00 per watt in Jamaica. The potential integration of off-grid solutions with the national grid is still under exploration, as hybrid systems could enhance energy supply reliability and resilience."

Environmentalists have long advocated for smart energy, and Jamaica is now embracing its benefits. According to an article in the *Jamaican Observer* titled "Time to rethink our energy infrastructure," in March 2024, Prime Minister Andrew Holness announced a new loan product for National Housing Trust contributors, offering smart home energy solutions such as solar panels, batteries, solar water heaters, and other renewable technologies like wind, hydropower, and biomass. Off-grid renewable energy plays a crucial role in Jamaica's energy transformation, as these systems can be installed more quickly and with lower capital costs compared to expanding the national grid.

Solar energy, in particular, is well-suited to Jamaica's sunny climate and can provide affordable electricity in areas with limited or no grid access. Beyond individual households, off-grid solutions support small businesses, clinics, schools, and other community-level services, fostering local economic growth. As noted by Small (2024), the Wolmer's Trust Group of Schools has equipped all three of its campuses with solar panels, yielding considerable advantages such as annual savings of $16 million. The installation of 954 panels across the prep, boys', and girls' schools has significantly lessened their dependence on the Jamaica Public Service (JPS) grid.

Policy and Institutional Reforms

While examining policies we must investigate the work of Feenstra's gender lens framework that looks at how these energy policies and various systems affect women, especially with accessing various energy sources during decision-making. She also explores the intersection that exists with gender, energy and social justice. Renewable energy can have a greater impact on women particularly women in low-income households in Jamaica, these barriers to accessing energy resources further exacerbate the inequalities that are placed on marginalized women. Therefore, we need to have greater improvement and greater gender inclusive policies as a means of reducing energy poverty in Jamaica by further empowering women and promoting greater social equity through sustainable energy initiatives (Feenstra, 2020). These policies could include:

Gender-Responsive Energy Policies: Developing and implementing policies that explicitly address the gender dimensions of energy access is crucial. This includes ensuring women's representation in energy policy-making bodies and designing programmes that target women's specific energy needs.

Financial Incentives: Providing subsidies, low-interest loans, and grants for renewable energy projects can encourage investment. Special financial products tailored for women entrepreneurs can help them start energy-related businesses, fostering both economic empowerment and energy access.

Capacity Building and Education

In 2017 the USAID CARCEP team trained several persons in Westmoreland looking at how best to utilise solar energy they were even certified by the Heart Trust institute... (Representative from the energy team, 2022)

Training and Education Programmes: Offering training programmes in renewable energy technologies for women can enhance their technical skills and employability. Educational campaigns that raise awareness about the benefits of clean energy and gender equality can shift societal attitudes and encourage more equitable practices.

STEM Education: Promoting science, technology, engineering, and mathematics (STEM) education among girls is vital for long-term gender equity. Encouraging young women to pursue careers in the energy sector can diversify the workforce and bring new perspectives to the industry.

Public-Private Partnerships

Collaborative Projects: Partnerships between the government, private sector, and non-governmental organizations can pool resources and expertise to implement large-scale energy projects. Ensuring these partnerships include gender-focused initiatives can maximize their impact on both energy access and gender equity.

Corporate Social Responsibility (CSR): Encouraging companies to adopt CSR practices that support renewable energy and gender equality can lead to innovative projects and investments. For instance, companies can sponsor training programmes for women in renewable energy or fund community-based energy projects.

It is equally necessary to remove the social and cultural barriers that prevent women from participating in assistance programmes. Indeed, it is vital to understand that energy demands differ by gender: women are far more exposed to the impacts of energy poverty than males. To achieve long-term success, energy policy must be redesigned. The issue extends beyond India; worldwide energy policy is frequently gender blind. Gender-neutral policies designed to provide equal chances do not necessarily provide equal results; thus, gender-sensitive policies are essential. A policy that recognizes the prevalent intra-household gender hierarchy, for example, will be more effective in ensuring that the household invests not only in solar lamps (which men are more likely to agree to) but also in solar cookers (which men may not directly benefit from because they spend less time in the kitchen).

Women must be considered not just as consumers of diverse energy services, but also as entrepreneurs, designers, and inventors who contribute to energy security (Pavithra, 2021). In Jamaica, addressing energy poverty and advancing gender equity necessitates a multidimensional strategy that incorporates policy reforms, capacity building, strategic partnerships, and the development of renewable energy. Through a focus on solutions that take gender dynamics and energy access into account, Jamaica can build a more sustainable and inclusive future. Encouraging women to work in the energy sector improves their socioeconomic standing and advances national development.

References

Duflo, E. (2012). Women empowerment and economic development. *Journal of Economic Literature, 50*(4), 1051–1079. https://doi.org/10.1257/jel.50.4.1051

ENERGIA. (2017). *The Gender and Energy Research Programme: Policy Brief #1.* https://www.energia.org/assets/2017/03/Policybrief-Energia-March-GERP-2017-final-lr.pdf

Feenstra, G. (2020). Gender and energy justice: A framework for policy development in the Caribbean. *Journal of Energy & Development, 46*(2), 145–163.

Gordon-Strachan, G., et al. (2014). Female gender is a social determinant of diabetes in the Caribbean. *International Journal of Environmental Research and Public Health, 11*(9), 9403–9412.

Indrawati, S. M. (2023). *6 Human capital development and gender equality in Indonesia*. Gender Equality and Diversity in Indonesia: Identifying Progress and Challenges, 93.
International Energy Agency (IEA). (2017). *World Energy Outlook 2017*. https://www.iea.org/reports/world-energy-outlook-2017
International Labour Organization (ILO). (2019). *ILOSTAT: Statistics on women*. https://ilostat.ilo.org/
International Energy Agency. (2022). https://www.iea.org/reports/renewables-2022
International Labour Organization. (2018). Greening with jobs: World Employment Social Outlook 2018. ILO.
International Labour Organization (2019). *Promoting employment opportunities for people with disabilities*. https://www.ilo.org/wcmsp5/groups/public/%2D%2D-ed_emp/%2D%2D-ifp_skills/documents/publication/wcms_735531.pdf
International Renewable Energy Agency. (2019). Renewable energy: A gender perspective. IRENA.
Jamaica Information Service (JIS). (2018). *Energy news*. https://jis.gov.jm/news/?category=energy
Laxmi, V., Parikh, J., Karmakar, S., & Dabrase, P. (2003). *Household energy, women's hardship and health impacts in rural Rajasthan, India: Need for sustainable energy solutions* (pp. 50–68). Energy for Sustainable Development. https://www.sciencedirect.com/science/article/pii/S0973082608600370
Middlemiss, L. (2022, July 1). Who is vulnerable to energy poverty in the Global North.... https://wires.onlinelibrary.wiley.com/doi/full/10.1002/wene.455
Munsell, M. (2017, April 4). *4 facts you should know about the Caribbean Solar Market*. Greentech Media. https://www.greentechmedia.com/articles/read/four-facts-you-should-know-about-the-caribbean-solar-market
Office of the Prime Minister. (2018, October 17). *Jamaica to increase renewables target to 50% – PM Holness*. JIS Jamaica. https://jis.gov.jm/jamaica-to-increase-renewables-target-to-50-pm-holness/
Organisation for Economic Co-operation and Development (OECD). (2018). *Gender equality*. https://www.oecd.org/en/topics/policy-issues/gender-equality.html
Pan American Health Organization (PAHO). (2018). *Gender equality in health*. https://www.paho.org/en/topics/gender-equality-health
Powell, L. (2016). Energy transition in a carbon consuming country: India. In R. Looney (Ed.), *Handbook of transitions to energy and climate security* (pp. 259–272). Routledge.
Renewable Energy Systems Training (REST). (2022). *K-12 Renewable Energy Workshop: Lecture Slides*. https://ate.is/index.php?ID=42314&P=FullRecord

Rose, D. (2024). *Wigton accelerating diversification: Shareholders to vote on name change as company eyes opportunities away from wind*. Jamaica Observer. https://www.jamaicaobserver.com/
Sen, A. (2001). *Development as freedom*. Oxford University Press.
Small, S. (2024, November 22). *Wolmer's group of Schools Reaps Big Savings from solar panels*. Lead Stories | Jamaica Gleaner. https://jamaica-gleaner.com/article/lead-stories/20241122/wolmers-group-schools-reaps-big-savings-solar-panels
Smith, L. C., & Haddad, L. (2015). Reducing child undernutrition: Past drivers and priorities for the post-MDG era. *World Development, 68*, 180–204. https://www.sciencedirect.com/science/article/pii/S0305750X14003834
Spiegel, S., & Schwank, O. (2022, May 27). *Bridging the "great finance divide" in developing countries*. Brookings. https://www.brookings.edu/articles/bridging-the-great-finance-divide-in-developing-countries/
United Nations Educational, Scientific and Cultural Organization (UNESCO). (2019). *Gender equality*. [Details not specified].
United Nations Development Programme (UNDP). (2022). *EnGenDER Highlights*. https://www.undp.org/barbados/engender-highlights
United Nations. (2021). *The Sustainable Development Goals Report 2021*. United Nations. https://unstats.un.org/sdgs/report/2021/The-Sustainable-Development-Goals-Report-2021.pdf
United Nations. (2022). *The Sustainable Development Goals Report 2022*. United Nations. https://unstats.un.org/sdgs/report/2022/The-Sustainable-Development-Goals-Report-2022.pdf
United Nations Department of Economic and Social Affairs. (2023). *The Sustainable Development Goals Report 2023: Special Edition*. United Nations. https://unstats.un.org/sdgs/report/2023/
United Nations Economic Commission for Latin America and the Caribbean (ECLAC). (2021). *Implications of gender roles in natural resource governance in Latin America and the Caribbean*. https://www.cepal.org/en/insights/implications-gender-roles-natural-resource-governance-latin-america-andcaribbean
World Bank. (2010). Education and health services in Latin America: The impact of women's education on child health. documents.worldbank.org/en/publication/documents-reports/documentdetail/884161468270311328/education-and-health-services-in-latin-america-the-impact-of-womens-education-on-child-health
World Bank Group. (2015, August 3). *In Rwanda, a brighter future for Miriam*. World Bank. https://www.worldbank.org/en/news/feature/2015/03/05/in-rwanda-a-brighter-future-for-miriam
World Bank Group. (2019, April 26). Improving energy efficiency and security in Jamaica. Results Briefs. https://www.worldbank.org/en/results/2019/04/26/improving-energy-efficiency-and-security-in-jamaica

Worldometer. (2023). *World population clock.* https://www.worldometers.info/world-population/

World Health Organization (WHO). (2018). *Gender equality in health.* https://www.paho.org/en/topics/gender-equality-health

World Health Organization (WHO). (2021). *Household air pollution and health.* https://www.who.int/news-room/fact-sheets/detail/household-air-pollution-and-health

World Health Organization (WHO). (2023). *Household air pollution and health.* [Details not specified].

World Health Organization (WHO) & United Nations Children's Fund (UNICEF). (2021). *Billions of people will lack access to safe water, sanitation and hygiene in 2030 unless progress quadruples.* https://armenia.un.org/en/134619-billions-people-will-lack-access-safe-water-sanitation-and-hygiene-2030-unlessprogress

CHAPTER 4

Implications of Having Affordable and Accessible Energy on Low-Income Households

Abstract This chapter delves more into investigating and highlighting the implications of having affordable and accessible energy on low-income households. The availability of affordable and accessible energy has the potential to significantly impact the lives of low-income households. In this chapter, we will explore the potential implications of having affordable and accessible energy on low-income households, including economic, health, environmental, and social impacts. These various perspectives look at the challenges regarding the use of renewable energy and its implication on Jamaica and other Caribbean countries. Gender-sensitive policies are keen to ensure that energy access and resources address the unique needs of low-income women. The chapter also speaks to the importance of ENERGIA which is an international network on gender and energy that highlighted the success of women from renewable energy projects from community-owned energy systems and the impact that these successes have had in reducing poverty within their community while empowering women.

Keywords ENERGIA • Gender sensitive policies • International network • Renewable energy projects

Energy is a fundamental requirement of every household, business, and industry. It is an essential part of human life, and without it, life becomes almost impossible. However, the cost of energy can be a significant burden on low-income households. In comparison to other families, low-income households globally spend a higher percentage of their income on home energy expenses (such as electricity, natural gas, and other home heating fuels). This metric is frequently called the "energy burden" on a household. According to a recent study, low-income households have three times the energy burden of other households ("Low-income Energy Affordability Data (LEAD) Tool," n.d.).

Regarding Jamaica in 2022, Dr. Nigel Clarke, Minister of Finance and the Public Service, declared that over 450,000 low- and middle-class households—who use up to 200 kWh of electricity each month—will receive a 20% bill-paying contribution during the following four months. The programme anticipated to mainly help those with lower incomes, such as vendors, security guards, housekeepers, domestic workers, bartenders, waiters, handypersons, and many other informal economy jobs, as well as hardworking Jamaicans making minimum wage or slightly more. It was made available under the government's proposed We CARE Energy Co-Pay Programme ("Jamaica Government to pay 20 percent of electricity bill for low-income households," 2022) (JIS, 2022).

The availability of affordable and accessible energy has the potential to significantly impact the lives of low-income households. In this chapter, we will explore the potential implications of having affordable and accessible energy on low-income households, including economic, health, environmental, and social impacts.

Economic Implications

Sign and Ru (2022) denoted that access to affordable and accessible energy can have significant economic implications for low-income households. Lower energy costs can free up resources that can be used for other necessities such as food, clothing, and education. This, in turn, can reduce poverty and increase economic stability for low-income households.

> I *would love to install solar but I can't afford it. I try by purchasing energy efficient lightbulbs etc. but I don't know as my bills are still very high.* (Focus group representative, 2022)

Access to affordable energy is a crucial factor in the socioeconomic development of any nation. In Jamaica, where many low-income households struggle with high energy costs and unreliable access, the introduction of renewable energy sources such as solar and wind power can catalyze significant economic opportunities. This not only improves household stability but also contributes to national economic growth. Jamaica's plentiful solar and wind resources present a great opportunity for the development of renewable energy. Using these resources generates a variety of job opportunities in addition to assisting in lowering the country's reliance on imported fossil fuels. Several important regions can see an increase in employment because of the renewable energy sector's growth:

1. Manufacturing: Setting up shops to produce solar panels, wind turbines, and other parts can lead to the creation of many jobs. These industrial facilities can help low-income people maintain their economic stability by giving them steady jobs.
2. Installation: Skilled labour is needed to install renewable energy systems, like wind turbines and solar panels. It is possible to create training programmes that will provide low-income people the skills they need to install these systems and open important job prospects for them.
3. Maintenance: To guarantee the effective operation of renewable energy systems, continuous maintenance is necessary. Low-income households can benefit from long-term employment in maintenance roles, which guarantees their continued access to the infrastructure supporting renewable energy sources.
4. Entrepreneurship: Low-income households may be encouraged to start their own businesses if they have access to inexpensive energy. For example, people can launch small enterprises that offer energy-related services like installing and maintaining solar panels. Increased economic activity and the creation of jobs within the community may result from this.
5. Economic Diversification: Jamaica's economy may become more diverse as a result of the expansion of the renewable energy industry. The nation can further increase economic stability and prosperity by reinvesting the money saved by lowering its dependency on imported fossil fuels.

Health Implications

Jamaica is very hot often and we utilise the fridge to keep us cool and I would love a little A.C. but me cant afford the AC or the JPS bill I will receive .... (Focus group representative, 2022)

Low-income households are more likely to experience health problems related to inadequate or insufficient energy. For instance, inadequate heating during winter can lead to hypothermia, pneumonia, and other respiratory illnesses. Also, according to the PAHO, 2023, The Pan American Health Organization (PAHO) relaunched a programme to eliminate 30 communicable illnesses and related ailments throughout the Americas. Many are well-known threats, such as tuberculosis (TB), HIV, and cervical cancer, but others are overlooked diseases that threaten vulnerable, marginalized, or inaccessible communities.

Moreover, low-income households are more likely to experience indoor air pollution due to the use of kerosene, coal, and other fossil fuels for heating and cooking. According to the Ministry of Health (2018), non-communicable diseases (NCDs) are the primary cause of mortality in Jamaica. In fact, four main NCDs—cancer, cardiovascular disease, diabetes, and chronic lower respiratory illness—are responsible for seven of every ten fatalities in Jamaica. This can cause respiratory problems, eye irritation, and other health problems.

However, access to affordable and accessible energy can significantly improve the health of low-income households. For instance, the use of clean energy sources such as solar and wind power can reduce indoor air pollution, thereby improving the respiratory health of household members ("Office of Energy Efficiency & Renewable Energy," n.d.). Moreover, access to reliable energy sources can ensure that households have adequate heating and cooling, thereby reducing the risk of hypothermia and heat stroke.

Environmental Implications

The use of fossil fuels for energy production is a significant contributor to greenhouse gas emissions, which are responsible for climate change. Low-income households are more likely to rely on fossil fuels for energy production, mainly because they cannot afford cleaner sources of energy. This makes them more vulnerable to the adverse effects of climate change such as floods, droughts, and extreme weather events.

However, access to affordable and accessible energy can significantly reduce the environmental impact of low-income households. The use of renewable energy sources such as solar and wind power can significantly reduce greenhouse gas emissions, thereby mitigating the adverse effects of climate change. Moreover, the use of clean energy sources can reduce air pollution, thereby improving the overall environmental quality of the community.

SOCIAL IMPLICATIONS

I know I pay for other people electricity bills on my own and this is a huge distraction as the cost is very high... (Focus group representative, 2002)

Access to inexpensive and accessible electricity can have serious societal consequences for low-income families ("The quality of life of individuals and societies is affected by energy choices," 2013). For example, using renewable energy sources can help low-income households gain energy independence, lessening their reliance on external energy sources. As a result, they may feel more independent and empowered. Moreover, access to affordable and accessible energy can improve the overall quality of life of low-income households ("How Renewable Energy Can Help Low Income," n.d.).

For instance, the use of renewable energy sources can provide households with access to electricity, which can improve their access to information, education, and communication. Thus, creating a gender-inclusive renewable energy business might enable women in rural regions to be both consumers and producers of clean energy, simplifying the transition to a greener, more sustainable future. Low-income women's lives and livelihoods suffer disproportionately from a lack of access to inexpensive, clean, and modern energy (Srivastav, 2022).

POLICY IMPLICATIONS

National energy policies and labour market patterns may exacerbate gender energy inequality. Such inequalities can be seen in the allocation of fossil fuel subsidies, and their consequences can be seen in women's access to transportation and land use. Subsidies for fossil fuel production, for example, frequently benefit more large energy producers, industries that have traditionally been dominated by men. Priority for energy access is frequently given in developing countries to large industrial, export-oriented activities, which are typically owned by men. According to 2018 statistics from 29 countries (22 IEA members), there are 76% fewer women than males working in the energy industry, which is a substantial divergence from the overall 8% gender gap. Despite the fact that women make up 47% of the entire national employment, they only account for 25% of energy workers (Ritchie, 2024).

Historically, energy policy has concentrated on technical challenges connected to supply security, such as fuel supply mix optimization. By focusing solely on the "supply-side," numerous "demand-side" concerns, such as end-user demands, priorities, and resources (such as skills and funding), are disregarded (Ministry of Energy Mozambique et al., 2012). A demand-side approach may identify that women are more disadvantaged than males in identical situations; for example, women have less access to and control over assets such as land, cash, and credit than men do. Women's technical abilities are frequently weaker than men's; for example, compared to males, women have lower reading levels and less expertise with hardware. Consequently, men can often gain access to "modern" energy forms more easily than women and hence men's activities tend to benefit from energy policy more.

Majority of policymakers are men. Males predominate in energy institutions and organizations, especially in professional roles. This holds true for the governmental and business sectors as well as for civil society (NGOs that deal with energy, for example). Many energy practitioners lack gender awareness because they do not completely comprehend how energy affects men and women differently (Ministry of Energy Mozambique et al., 2012).

The absence of consideration for gender in energy policy often impacts women's access to vital technology and resources for their own empowerment and well-being. This means that in order to meet women's demands in energy policy, officials must increase their understanding of gender problems and develop their capacity to implement gender mainstreaming. A policymaker who is sensitive to gender issues is able to comprehend how a given initiative, programme, or policy will affect both men and women.

Moreover, a planner who considers gender may carry out policies, initiatives, and projects with consideration for gender. When programmes, projects, and policies are gender-aware, they take into account the distinct requirements of men and women in terms of both content and procedure.

Gender-sensitive policies are keen to ensure that energy access and resources address the unique needs of low-income women. As presented the policies should prioritize the involvement in energy decision-making and providing renewable energy technologies that can significantly improve social and economic relations. ENERGIA is an international network on gender and energy that highlights women's success from renewable energy projects from community-owned energy systems and their impact on reducing poverty within their community while empowering women. Women still maintain the "triple burden" within their community and they have to manage technologies with regard to cooking the food, and access to energy in domestic services. Jamaica like many other countries in the Global South also needs to ensure that when these policies are implemented they are effectively utilized therefore giving women and children better access to affordable, clean, and sustainable energy bringing more women into the process and also promoting sustainable development.

Several countries have also implemented gender-specific energy policies that incorporate gender-sensitive approaches that have proven effective in supporting women, these include the Gender Mainstreaming the Economic Community of West African States (ECOWAS) that looks at Gender Mainstreaming Policy for Energy. This therefore gives women a voice and promotes equitable energy access while reducing energy poverty (National Renewable Energy Laboratory NREL, 2019). ENERGIA (2020) also highlights women's involvement in countries like Ghana, Tanzania, and Rwanda's increase in women's participation in the energy business and how renewable energy is distributed. It also demonstrates how low-income women have had to reinvest in trying to improve their health, education, and welfare (ENERGIA, 2020). Greater support for energy-efficient technologies also helps women save time on household chores and can generate more effort in income-generating activities. These policies also showcase how women can be transformed into gender roles while improving economic independence. (ENERGIA, 2020).

Renewable Energy Promotes Equity

The availability of renewable energy sources in Jamaica, along with the adoption of decentralized energy systems, holds considerable promise for reducing energy poverty among low-income women. Although Jamaica has begun to embrace renewable energy through solar, wind, and hydropower initiatives, challenges related to energy poverty remain, especially in rural areas that are often neglected. Implementing decentralized solutions like community solar microgrids or individual household solar systems could ensure consistent and affordable energy access for these communities, specifically catering to the needs of low-income women.

For numerous women, energy poverty intensifies pre-existing inequalities, restricting their chances for education, job opportunities, and entrepreneurial ventures. Having dependable access to energy could significantly alter these situations by facilitating economic activities, decreasing the time dedicated to labour-intensive household tasks, and enhancing access to vital services such as education and healthcare. Furthermore, UN Women (2015) believes that "decentralized energy systems can empower women through community ownership models where they play an active role in decision-making and system maintenance, thereby promoting leadership and technical skills."

Establishing cooperatives allows women to take on leadership or co-management positions in decentralized energy initiatives, such as solar mini-grids or community wind farms. This approach guarantees that women participate in decision-making and benefit economically from these projects. Furthermore, providing access to microfinance loans and grants specifically aimed at women can facilitate investments in renewable energy technologies, including solar home systems and small-scale biogas plants. These financial products should be customized to meet the needs of women, offering flexible repayment terms to enhance accessibility and practicality.

For example, supported by $120 million in funding from the World Bank (2015), the Rwanda Electricity Access Scale-Up and Sector Wide Approach Development Project facilitates access to reliable and affordable electricity for Rwandans. This initiative has led to the construction of 1650 kilometres of transmission and distribution lines, increasing electricity availability for more citizens of Rwanda (The World Bank Group, In Rwanda, a Brighter Future for Miriam, 2015). This initiative supports the inclusion of women in biogas programmes, providing subsidies for household biogas plants and training women on their operation and maintenance.

Reliable access to energy might change the lives of many women in Jamaica if the government adopts the Rwandan blueprint. Energy poverty exacerbates already-existing disparities by restricting opportunities for entrepreneurship, education, and employment. Through facilitating economic activity, cutting down on time spent on tiresome household tasks, and enhancing access to basic amenities like healthcare and education.

Through community ownership models, where women actively participate in maintenance and decision-making, decentralized systems can help empower women by developing their technical and leadership abilities.

The effectiveness of energy systems that prioritize energy justice relies heavily on their ownership and governance frameworks. To ensure equitable benefits, projects must incorporate inclusive design principles that emphasize accessibility, affordability, and active community participation. For instance, to prevent economic exclusion, it is essential to offer subsidies or financing options to low-income households. Additionally, participatory governance models can ensure that the voices of women and other marginalized groups are acknowledged and considered. When decentralized renewable energy systems are integrated into a framework that emphasizes social justice, equitable access, and community empowerment, they have the potential to alleviate energy poverty among low-income women in Jamaica.

References

ENERGIA Group. (2020). *Energia Group's top news stories of 2020*. https://www.energiagroup.com/newsmedia/energia-groups-top-new-stories-of-2020/

Jamaica Information Service. (2022). *Government to pay 20 per cent of electricity bill for low-income households*. https://jis.gov.jm/government-to-pay-20-per-cent-of-electricity-bill-for-low-income-households/

Ministry of Energy Mozambique, & Partners. (2012). *Mozambique's ambitious energy strategy at 'golden moment' in the fight against poverty*. https://www.worldbank.org/en/news/feature/2012/04/04/mozambiques-ambitious-energy-strategy-at-golden-moment-in-the-fight-against-poverty

Ministry of Health & Wellness. (2018). *Vitals – A quarterly report of the Ministry of Health (May 2018)*. https://www.moh.gov.jm/data/vitals-a-quarterly-report-of-the-ministry-of-health-may-2018/

National Renewable Energy Laboratory. (2019). [*Title of the report*]. [URL]

Ritchie, C. (2024, February 2). *Women in the energy industry*. SaveOnEnergy.com. https://www.saveonenergy.com/resources/women-in-energy/

Sign, D., & Ru, X. (2022). Gender and energy: Exploring the intersection of gender and energy access. *Energy Research & Social Science, 87*, 102541. https://doi.org/10.1016/j.erss.2022.102541

Srivastav Energy Economist, S. (2022, April 12). *How clean energy can empower women in rural communities*. International Growth Centre. https://www.theigc.org/blogs/gender-equality/how-clean-energy-can-empower-women-rural-communities

Sunrun. (n.d.). *How renewable energy can help low income communities.* https://www.sunrun.com/go-solar-center/renewable-energy-helps-low-income-communities

The CLEAN Network. (2013). *The quality of life of individuals and societies is affected by energy choices.* https://cleanet.org/clean/literacy/energy7.html

UN Women. (2015). *Gender equality, women's empowerment and climate change.* https://www.unwomen.org/en/news/in-focus/climate-change/2015

U.S. Department of Energy. (n.d.). *Low-Income Energy Affordability Data (LEAD) Tool.* https://www.energy.gov/indianenergy/low-income-energy-affordability-data-lead-tool

U.S. Department of Energy, Office of Energy Efficiency & Renewable Energy. (n.d.). *About the Office of Energy Efficiency & Renewable Energy.* Retrieved May 11, 2025, from https://www.energy.gov/eere/about-office-energy-efficiency-and-renewable-energy

World Bank Group. (2015, August 3). *In Rwanda, a brighter future for Miriam.* World Bank. https://www.worldbank.org/en/news/feature/2015/03/05/in-rwanda-a-brighter-future-for-miriam

CHAPTER 5

Global Implication of Gender and Energy Poverty

Abstract This chapter further investigates the role of energy not just on Jamaica but also from a global perspective. It also spends more time by looking at the various gender roles and how they also utilize energy from a primary perspective. The chapter also investigates how female-headed households and business also benefit. Based on these assumptions it also looks further at how the Caribbean is also benefitting with these energy uses and how the use of more renewable energy would affect the production of women and the impact this has on the economics, social, and health of these females. This chapter also provides a quantitative assessment of the use of electricity especially in these single-headed households and the impact it has on the family and the community along with the type of usage of electricity. Special discussion is centred around disabled women, youth, and minority women which also showcases the impact of energy usage on these individuals.

Keywords Renewable energy • Electricity • Disabled women • Youth and minority women

© The Author(s), under exclusive license to Springer Nature Switzerland AG 2025
S. Walters, *Energy Poverty Among Women in Jamaica's Low-Income Communities*, https://doi.org/10.1007/978-3-031-89079-6_5

Energy Poverty in the Caribbean

In the Caribbean, where many people lack dependable and reasonably priced access to modern energy services, energy poverty is a serious problem. This problem lowers the general quality of life, exacerbates inequality, and impedes economic progress. Guevara et al. (2023) define energy poverty as the inability to obtain electricity and reliance on the conventional heating and cooking methods of biomass. Lack of access to contemporary energy services, such as electricity, is known as energy poverty. As was said in the previous chapter, it is a complicated problem that has an impact on social well-being, public health, and economic growth. A significant portion of the population lacks access to fairly priced and reliable energy services in many Caribbean countries, which is characterized by high levels of energy poverty. With reference to scholarly research and statistical data, this chapter will analyse the consequences of energy poverty in the Caribbean, emphasizing its effects on gender.

Several Caribbean countries experience energy poverty to varying degrees, where significant portions of their populations lack reliable and affordable access to modern energy services. In Haiti, only around 40% of people have access to electricity, and each individual uses an average of about 21 Kilowatt-hours (KWH) annually ("Privacy Sheild Framework," n.d.). Reliability varies, even for people who have access to energy. Diesel generators are necessary for many businesses and larger homes due to their unreliability.

Global corporations have voiced discontent with Haiti's high energy costs in the industrial and commercial sectors when compared to other nations in the region in which they operate. In addition to impeding investment and the growth of profitable enterprises, the unavailability of reasonably priced and dependable power lowers residential consumers' standards of living. According to Maertens and Stork (2017), charcoal continues to be the fuel of choice for food preparation in many Haitian rural homes, which is a major contributor to deforestation. An estimated 4 million metric tons (MT) of wood products are consumed annually by Haitians, of which approximately one-third is converted into charcoal to satisfy urban customers' demand for cooking fuel (U.S Agency for International Development, 2017).

The effects of the climate and economic crises put over 40% of Dominicans in precarious situations and at risk of becoming impoverished. Similarly, women experience poverty at higher rates due to differences in employment and income between the sexes, shorter working lifespans, more unemployment, and unpaid work (World Bank Group, 2024). To achieve its energy demands, the Dominican Republic is mostly dependent on imported fossil fuels. The nation's reliance on oil exposes it to fluctuations in the world market price, resulting in costly and unstable energy expenses. There are still areas of energy poverty in the Dominican Republic even though there is widespread access to electricity. The cost of power can be exorbitant for low-income families, which causes problems for many households with regard to energy affordability. Furthermore, some areas may have sporadic supply of energy or rely on antiquated infrastructure that causes frequent outages even though they have access to it (Barnes & Samad, 2018; Douglas & Hussain, 2018).

Due to a lack of adequate energy infrastructure, Jamaica has the greatest energy poverty ranking among the 82 low-to-middle-income nations with high rates of energy poverty (Marsh, 2023). Marsh (2023) also added that, the main source of energy production in Jamaica is fossil fuels, especially oil. These sources provide for about 89% of all energy, with renewables bringing up 11% overall and solar for just 1%. Oil prices are high in Jamaica since the majority of the country's oil is imported. In 2010, the profit from items exported was less than the cost of imported oil by over 118%. Therefore, using fossil fuels indefinitely is not sustainable for the environment or the economics of the nation. With the construction of small modular nuclear reactors for the generation of clean energy, the government of Jamaica, according to Prime Minister Andrew Holness, plans to reduce prices and eradicate energy poverty. Going nuclear will enable Jamaicans to obtain more inexpensive power to improve their quality of life, according to Holness, who observed that the costs of electricity and energy poverty are big burdens for the country's citizens (McKenzie, 2023).

Gender Roles

According to (Evans, 1999), "Gender has grown to have a variety of overlapping meanings, and it appears that this definition is still changing. First, it alludes to the social division between masculinity and femininity or maleness and femaleness. Instead of being based on the biological differences between men and women, this separation is socially generated through interpersonal relationships. The idea of gender is also sometimes used to describe a characteristic shared by all people, namely whether they are male or female. Some people now confuse gender and sex because of this second definition of gender." While gender is a societal construct that defines what is feminine and what is masculine, sex—whether female or male—is determined by biology. Gender roles are influenced by variables like education and economy and are acquired rather than natural.

Equality between men, women, girls, and boys has been a goal of the United Nations since its inception. The 1945 UN Charter includes the objective "to reaffirm faith in fundamental human rights, in the dignity and worth of the human person, in the equal rights of men and women and of all nations large and small." According to a UNICEF Situational Analysis on Gender Disparities in Jamaica 2007 Report:

> *The equal enjoyment of rights, opportunities, services, and resources by women, men, boys, and girls is defined as gender equality. "When boys, girls, women, and men all have equal opportunities to fulfill their potential and contribute to the political, economic, and social advancement of society while also sharing in the benefits, then gender equality has been achieved."*

Now, according to the most recent Jamaica Survey of Living Conditions, households headed by women continue to have more dependants than those headed by men ("Women continue to head most Jamaican families with children," 2014). According to a poll conducted in 2012, 46.4% of all homes were headed by women, and these households had a higher percentage of children. Also, among female-headed households, those with children and no man present took the largest share at 53.4%.

Households headed by males reflected larger proportions of persons in the working age group at 66.7% while 10.6% were dependent elderly men.

We learn what it is to be a man or a woman, how to behave, and how to interact with people through the gender system. Even if it has gotten better over time, certain areas, like Jamaica, still present more challenges. Women's exclusion from leadership roles and decision-making positions has been a problem that has to be eradicated from our culture; however, this differs depending on the nation, education, and religion.

One of the biggest issues in the region is frequently identified as violence against women, with Jamaica being utilized as a model nation for interventions due to the country's notably high rates of gender-based violence. However, Mohammed & Hashish, (2015) noted that the island's failings in terms of equality are more closely related to poverty, which allows gangs to develop in urban areas, the majority of the population lacks access to education, and a stunted social structure that promotes inequality than they are to any innate sexism. More than 1 in 4 women between the ages of 15 and 64 reported having suffered physical and/or sexual abuse from an intimate partner at some point in their lives, according to the 2016 Women's Health Survey, which put Jamaica's prevalence of gender-based violence at 27.8% (Statistical Institute of Jamaica et al., 2018).

Adverse childhood experiences (ACEs) are associated with gender-based violence in both men and women, and the Caribbean has a remarkably high ACE incidence (Adisa, 2020). According to surveys conducted by UN Women, 46% of Caribbean women report having been victims of violence at least once in their lives. Guyana and Jamaica are two very serious situations.

In most households in Jamaica there is a single parent in charge, normally the mother, who tends to be very young (between ages 15 and 19). This contrasts with year 2000 where the average American woman having her first baby was almost 25 years old. In 1970 the average age was 21.4 years for a first birth, according to a new report from the Centre for Disease Control and Prevention, today (more recent times) the average (or mean) age of mothers for birth is now age 27.2.

It can be agreed upon that many children in Jamaica do not have a good example and grow up believing that these behaviours (having children as a teenager) are normal and appropriate because after all, there is no one to tell them otherwise. Headly (2021) asserted, even the slightest engagement of Jamaican males in their children's life is commended. In addition, our women face social disgrace and humiliation for being unable to ignore their responsibilities and the numerous financial barriers that prevent them from doing so.

The consequences of fatherless households during adolescence are enormous because these kids are more likely to encounter the negative impacts of poverty. One of the biggest societal issues of our day is fatherlessness. It is well known that fatherlessness can have a long-lasting negative impact on children. They have a higher chance of becoming impoverished, quitting school, developing a drug addiction, having an unmarried child, or serving time in jail ("A Father's Impact on Child Development," 2023).

In our tertiary institutions we can also see this similarity effects, at UWI Mona, from 2010/11 to 2015/16, the average enrolment proportion was 67.6% female compared to 32.4% male; similarly, the graduation percentages are comparable (Policy Planning Development and Evaluation Division, the Research Unit, 2018).

According to Beuermann et al. (2024), in truth boys conduct the majority of child crimes, which is frequently the outcome of early gender indoctrination, increased exposure to violence, and school dropout rates. This explains why they are so heavily represented in prisons and other penal facilities; 183 boys were among the 235 minors imprisoned in 2006. Boys are often admitted for the following offenses: theft and breaking into stores (12%), injuring (12%), risky drug usage (11%) being unruly (9.3%), and unlawful firearm possession. In the same time frame, females were mostly hospitalized for care and protection (21%) followed by being unruly (17%), injuring, assault, and violating probation orders (4% each) ("The State of the World's Children 2007 and The Global Development, UNICEF," 2007).

Early childhood specialists seem to agree that parents are paying greater attention to their daughters, considered more fragile, and in need of greater protection, than their sons of the same age ("Transforming the Workforce for Children Birth Through Age 8: A Unifying Foundation," 2015).

In comparison to similar countries, the Caribbean area has made significant strides in obtaining universal primary school attendance and equivalent levels of educational attainment. However, as students go from basic to secondary and postsecondary school, persistent learning disparities continue throughout their lives. In addition, boys are falling behind in terms of educational achievement due to widening gender inequalities (Cao & Ng, 2023). Gaining a deeper understanding of the factors that shape this reality is crucial since failing to do so might result in long-term productivity disparities that impede optimal growth.

In addition to the general persistence of learning disparities across the course of a student's life, a new study shows that girls are increasingly outperforming boys in terms of learning outcomes. While elementary school enrolment and completion rates are comparable for boys and girls, females outnumber boys in secondary school completion rates. In terms of enrolling in postsecondary education, women do better than men do, and men are far more likely to belong to the group of people who are not in employment, education, or training (NEETs). Additionally, women routinely outperform men in learning accomplishment at the elementary, secondary, and postsecondary school levels in Caribbean nations, and this disparity is seen in all socioeconomic categories (Beuermann et al., 2023).

Children are "typically" clearly instructed on behaviour depending on gender and what is deemed "appropriate" or "not appropriate." According to the Gender Schema Theory, teenagers learn about gender norms and expectations purely via observation of their environment. The Gender Schema theory is a cognitive theory that explains how gender development happens through an information processing method (International Encyclopaedia of the Social & Behavioural Sciences, 2001).

The cognitive representation known as a schema serves as the foundation for this approach. A schema is a type of organizational framework that makes fresh information easier to understand and classify. Upon acquiring awareness of the societal norms regarding men and women, children will proactively search out information regarding the roles and characteristics that are seen suitable for each gender. After then, it's likely that the youngster would act in certain ways and make choices depending on how they perceive their gender. Moreover, the little learner will comprehend any fresh knowledge about gender from her or his surroundings. For example, it's possible for a child to see that her mother does most of the household tasks and childcare. She may also notice that her father doesn't help much with household maintenance and spends much of his time at work. As a result, this youngster may grow up with a gender schema that views males as the primary breadwinners and women as domestic help. She has, in a sense, absorbed gender roles—that is, the traits, actions, and perspectives that society deems proper for men and women. Based on these gender roles, the youngster may further infer that men are dominating, forceful, independent, and powerful, whereas women are innately docile, cooperative, fragile, and emotional. The child's adoption of gender stereotypes—broad generalizations about the traits and behaviours that men and women share—is reflected in this deduction. Gender norms and stereotypes are thus passed down from one generation to the next.

Edd Hoominfar (2021) posits that the main "agents of gender socialization," including family, educational institutions, peer groups, and the media, significantly influence how people perceive women. Depending on their child's gender, parents usually have preconceived notions about how they should behave. They also express, whether directly or indirectly, how they see other individuals. Kids take up the beliefs of their parents, and if discrimination against women was common in their home, they may end up endorsing it themselves. The negative perception of women is also influenced by the media's and advertising's emphasis on women's often exaggerated femininity and sexuality, emotional instability, and lack of independence.

Children get their earliest exposure to gender norms through their parents. For sons, fathers serve as role models, and for daughters, moms serve as role models. Parents anticipate that boys and girls will differ in personality traits and abilities based on their gender. In many respects, parents perpetuate these gender-specific norms. Hoominfar (2021) also added, play is one method that parents can use to help their children learn about gender norms. Their selection of toys is one illustration of this. For instance, girls are usually given dolls and kitchen sets, while boys are usually given sports equipment and toy automobiles. Girls' play is supposed to be more passive, and boys' play is supposed to be more active. For instance, boys are usually expected to battle, while girls to play tea parties.

Female-Headed Households and Businesses

According to Duncan-Price et al. (2021), gender roles and the opinions of Jamaican women paint an intriguing picture. Even among women who hold more modern conceptions of gender roles, some deeply ingrained conventional notions about the roles of men and women are part of Jamaican culture. This emphasizes how nuanced and intricate attitudes regarding gender roles are. Women continue to believe that men should be the natural heads of families and that it is a woman's duty to take care of her home, even though they reject more coercive ideas such as sexual obligation and obedience to their partners and embrace positive beliefs like shared authority in the home and the right of women to make their own financial decisions.

Social norms that uphold gender inequality act as obstacles to women's and girls' full enjoyment of their rights as equals and their potential as change-agents for the economy, society, and sustainable development. Women are more likely to get unequal compensation for equivalent work when they are underrepresented in positions of authority and decision-making (Gould et al., 2016). Additionally, women-owned businesses are more likely to face economic disadvantages and be denied equal opportunities to compete for business prospects. Women are also more likely to be the victims of sexual and physical assault. Over one in four Jamaican women, or 28% of all women, report having ever been the victim of intimate partner abuse or sexual assault ("UN Women's Health Survey," 2018). Due to social and economic stress brought on by the COVID-19 pandemic, movement restrictions, and social isolation policies, gender-based violence has skyrocketed.

Not all female-headed households are poor, and the evidence (statistics) suggests a link between antecedent factors and economic situation of households headed by women. However, according to Mokate, 2004, it was found in a shelter sector study carried out in Kingston, Jamaica, that female-headed households had a higher incidence of poverty and higher levels of hunger than male-headed households. Nyandoro (2024) asserted that poverty rates for female-headed households have declined over the years, but they still have a higher chance of falling into poverty than male-headed households.

Female-Headed Business

In Jamaica, the percentage of women in managerial roles has increased to 59.3% in recent years; nevertheless, just 33.0% of senior executives are female. Women own 38.2% of enterprises (Duncan-Price et al., 2021). Gender disparities have restricted women's access to capital for their enterprises, posing new obstacles and difficulties for female entrepreneurs. This is not exclusive to Jamaica; it is a global phenomenon. According to a 2014 survey by the Inter-American Development Bank's Multilateral Investment Fund (MIF), women entrepreneurs in the Latin American and Caribbean (LAC) countries primarily obtained financial backing for their enterprises from their spouses or relatives. Additional funding sources included personal savings and, in some situations, loans from the Caribbean Development Bank (CDB), which allows women to qualify for loans intended only for enterprises owned by women.

The listings on the Jamaica Junior Stock Exchange (JSE) serve to illustrate how it is clearly visible to the public that men dominate the business scene. Only 3 of the 49 public firms now listed on the JSE are run by women: Honey Bun, Image Plus Consultants, and Limners and Bards. This indicates that women lead just 6% of the JSE's listed businesses (Bryan, 2023). This is intriguing, especially after doing more research and discovering that, although the C-level of all these firms is mostly male (94%), the corporate structure of each of these organizations is at least 80% female. It is interesting to note that, in contrast to males, just 63.6% of women are employed, which surprised me. Despite recent increases to 59.3% of women in management roles in Jamaica (Brayan, 2023), women still make up just 33% of senior executives (ILO, 2018) and 38.2% of all enterprises are owned by women (Saner & Yiu, 2019).

Just 23% of micro-, small-, and medium-sized firms (MSMEs) in the Caribbean are owned by women. Despite women's critical involvement in economic growth and recovery, this data demonstrates the substantial gender disparity in business ownership within the region. According to IDB INVEST (2022), businesses run or owned by women are more likely to depend on short-term loans. According to our data, women-owned or led businesses have accessed about 20% of all short-term credit issued in each country over the past 20 years (loans with a maturity less than three years). These consist of credit cards, overdraft protection, and credit lines. Notably, within the same time frame, they only applied for 1.3% of medium-to-long term loans. The cost of borrowing is also typically greater for these short-term securities.

How Is the Caribbean Affected by Energy Poverty

Although there has been progress, the environmentally sound aspect is still far from being applicable for the majority of them. Nearly 2.7 billion people, or 40% of the global population, are estimated to lack access to clean cooking facilities worldwide, and instead rely on fuels like solid biomass, coal, or kerosene—all of which are known to be the most polluting energy sources.

Since energy, particularly in the form of electricity, is essential to the modern economy, it is a prerequisite for both social and economic advancement. Hirsh & Koomey (2015) posits that, there is still a significant correlation between economic growth and electricity demand. Energy security, or the continuous availability of energy sources at a reasonable cost, is therefore essential. Energy security has two indivisible components. The first is the long-term component, which is defined by the requirement for timely investments in order to deliver energy in accordance with environmental requirements and economic changes. The energy system's resilience, or the capacity to respond quickly to abrupt shifts in the supply-demand balance, is the second short-term factor. Resilience is the capacity of the system to withstand shocks and bounce back. Energy poverty in the Caribbean has far-reaching effects that influence all elements of life, including economic stability, social fairness, health, and environmental sustainability. The main consequences of energy poverty in the Caribbean are—(1) Economic impacts, (2) Social inequality, (3) Health risk, and (4) Environmental degradation.

ECONOMIC IMPACTS

Sustainable energy is necessary to fulfil the Sustainable Development Goals (SDGs), to which the Caribbean region and the rest of the world have committed. (i.e. RE choices and integrated energy efficiency measures). But now, fossil fuel-based energy sources—which are by definition non-renewable and unsustainable—provide the great bulk of the world's and the region's energy supply. Energy poverty has significant economic implications for countries in the Caribbean such as high energy prices. For instance, during the pandemic, when oil prices were rising globally, the Caribbean's already high energy costs increased much more. Caribbean households were impacted by this, particularly the poorest ones, as it further reduced their income. Prices for energy increased to over 50% in 2022 and then began to decline in 2023 and 2024 ("AskWBCaribbean: Talking Energy, Finding Solutions," 2022).

SOCIAL INEQUALITY

Energy poverty can also have significant social implications for people living in the Caribbean. Lack of access to reliable and affordable energy can limit opportunities for social and economic mobility, particularly for vulnerable populations such as women and children. For example, women in rural areas may spend several hours a day collecting firewood for cooking and heating, limiting their ability to participate in other economic activities or pursue education. Children may also miss school to help with household tasks such as collecting firewood, limiting their educational opportunities. The social inequality for energy poverty will result in time poverty. According to Jagoe et al. (2020), time poverty prevents women from participating in political, social, and educational activities as well as paid jobs, which feeds the cycle of economic poverty, gender inequity, and the never-ending drudgery trap. The preparation and acquisition of fuel, together with extended cooking sessions on inefficient and environmentally harmful stoves, provide a substantial time burden for women residing in communities that rely on biomass fuel and conventional cookstoves.

Health Risk

Health wise, one of the most immediate consequences of energy poverty is exposure to indoor air pollution, which results from burning solid fuels such as wood, charcoal, and kerosene for cooking and heating. According to the World Health Organization (2024), an estimated 3.2 million fatalities annually, including over 237,000 deaths of children under the age of five, were attributed to household air pollution in 2020. And also, every year, 6.7 million premature deaths are attributed to the combined impacts of home and ambient air pollution. In the Caribbean, many households rely on these solid fuels for cooking, and as a result, the region has some of the highest rates of indoor air pollution in the world.

The World Health Organization (2024) states that exposure to indoor air pollution can cause a range of health problems, including respiratory infections, heart disease, stroke, and lung cancer. These health problems disproportionately affect vulnerable populations, such as children, the elderly, and people with pre-existing health conditions. For example, in Trinidad and Tobago, a study found that children under the age of five who were exposed to indoor air pollution were more likely to suffer from acute respiratory infections.

Environmental Impacts

There are major environmental consequences associated with energy poverty in the Caribbean. The area is extremely susceptible to the effects of climate change, and many nations are already feeling the consequences of increased frequency and intensity of storms, rising sea levels, and other climate-related phenomena (Lindwall, 2022). In the Caribbean, the continuous use of non-renewable energy sources is a factor in environmental deterioration.

Haiti is suffering a major deforestation crisis, which has disastrous impacts on the country's ecology, economy, and people. During this time, Haiti lost all primary forest from 42 of its 50 highest and largest mountains (Hedges et al., 2018). Dependence on fossil fuels contributes to greenhouse gas emissions, which are a significant contributor to climate change. In addition, burning solid fuels for cooking and heating contributes to local air pollution, which can have serious health and environmental impacts.

Jamaica and Energy Poverty

In Jamaica, energy poverty is a serious problem that has a big impact on social cohesion, environmental sustainability, and economic stability. This study looks at the various effects of energy poverty in Jamaica, such as how it affects public health, education, economic development, and environmental degradation. Developing nations face significant obstacles due to energy poverty, which is defined as insufficient availability of cost-effective and dependable energy services. Energy poverty has a profound impact on many facets of life in Jamaica, a country that is mostly dependent on imported fossil fuels. To comprehend these effects and their significance for Jamaica's overall growth, this section of the chapter will examine these ramifications.

Jamaica Public Service Role in Energy Poverty—Monopolization

Figure 5.1 shows that 95% of the respondents get their energy from JPS. Given that this corporation is the only energy supplier in the nation and that this number represents most responses, it is easy to argue that this is a type of monopolization. In the Caribbean, including Jamaica, the

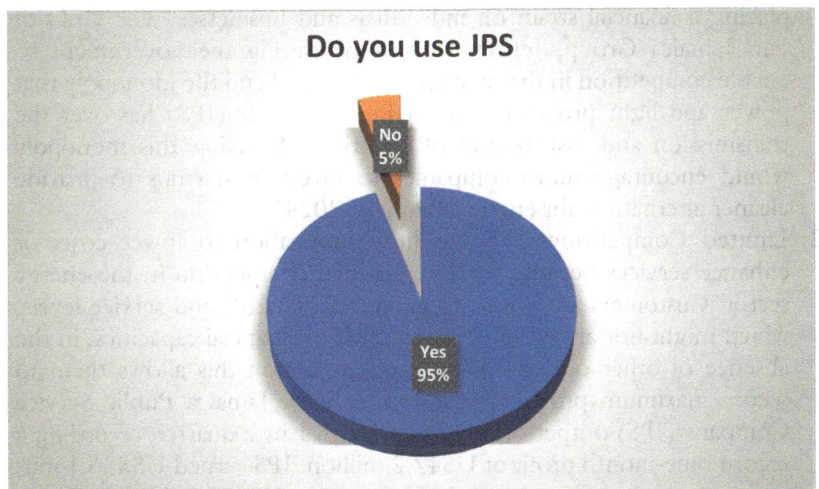

Fig. 5.1 Represents the number of respondents who currently use the Services of JPS

reliance on diesel and costly imported oil for electricity generation has led to some of the highest electricity prices globally. This reliance significantly impacts regional economic growth and creates challenges for local industries trying to compete with US counterparts. In Jamaica, the Jamaica Public Service Company (JPS) is the primary utility provider responsible for electricity generation and distribution. The company's dependence on imported fossil fuels, such as diesel, contributes to the high cost of electricity. This situation exacerbates economic challenges by increasing operational expenses for businesses and reducing their competitiveness in the global market. As a result, the high cost of electricity hinders economic development and growth prospects within the region.

With a monopoly (100 years) on the production, transmission, and distribution of power on the island, the Jamaica Public Service Company (JPS) is a major player in the energy industry of the island. The following are some consequences of this monopolistic control on energy poverty in Jamaica:

1. High Electricity Prices: JPS's monopolistic position as the only supplier of electricity allows it to establish high rates, which raises the cost of electricity. Because many residents find it impossible to purchase even basic electrical needs, these high costs exacerbate energy poverty by placing a financial strain on individuals and businesses. The CEO of Pan Jamaica Group, Jeffrey Hall, is pressuring the government to enable competition in that market segment and end the monopoly that power and light provider Jamaica Public Service (JPS) has over the transmission and distribution of electricity. Breaking this monopoly would encourage more companies to invest in startups to provide cleaner alternatives for energy (Bennett, 2024).
2. Limited Competition: JPS has little motivation to lower costs or enhance services because there is minimal competition in the energy sector. Customers are forced to accept JPS's tariffs and service levels, which might not always meet their needs or financial capacities, in the absence of other options. With no competition this allows them to secure maximum profit all year round. Last, Jamaica Public Service Company (JPS) outperformed the prior year by a quarter, recording a record nine-month profit of U$47.2 million. JPS earned US$36.1 million in profit in its fiscal year 2021, up from US$31 million in 2020. Additionally, the company's sales increased dramatically, coming in at

US$973 million as opposed to $888.7 million in 2020 (JPS makes record profit from summer, 2023).
3. Investment in Renewable Energy: The integration of renewable energy sources may be impacted by the monopolistic structure. JPS may be slowing down the adoption of renewable technologies, which could otherwise reduce energy costs and increase sustainability, due to its concentration on sustaining its current revenue streams and infrastructure.
4. Dependability and Service Quality: Monopolies can occasionally cause complacency in the provision of services. Concerns about irregular service and frequent power outages in Jamaica can be linked to the absence of competitive pressure on JPS to improve its operations or make investments in new infrastructure. In 2020, the Office of Utilities and Regulations (OUR) contacted JPS over plethora of complaints from customers. Over the last three months, the Office of Utilities Regulation (OUR) has received an increased number of complaints about excessive electricity bills. Elizabeth Bennett-Marsh 2022, a Public Education Specialist at the OUR, reported a 209% rise in complaints filed by phone, letter, and email with the regulator.

CONSEQUENCES OF ENERGY POVERTY IN JAMAICA

Economic Consequences

One of the most immediate and visible consequences of energy poverty in Jamaica is its economic impact. The high cost of electricity, largely due to the country's reliance on imported fossil fuels, places a significant financial burden on households and businesses. Jamaican consumers face some of the highest electricity prices in the world, which hampers economic growth and stifles entrepreneurial activity. Ironically, Fig. 5.2 reveals that 85% of respondents were not satisfied with their monthly service charge from JPS. However, 15% of respondents said they were satisfied with the monthly charge. Conversely, the 16% difference between these two responses reflects the economic costs of energy poverty in Jamaica.

Small- and medium-sized enterprises (SMEs), which are critical to the Jamaican economy, are particularly affected. High energy costs reduce profit margins, making it difficult for these businesses to expand or invest

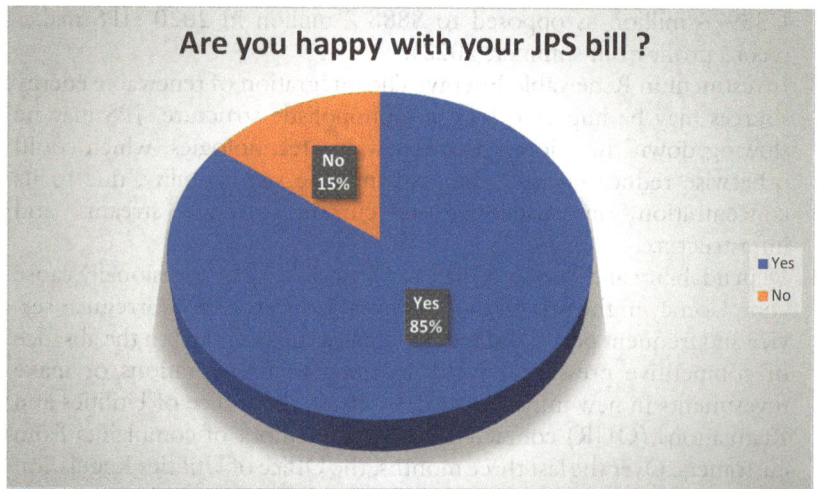

Fig. 5.2 Represents the number of respondents who are happy with their JPS bill (monthly)

in new technologies. This, in turn, limits job creation and economic development, perpetuating a cycle of poverty and economic stagnation.

Additionally, energy poverty exacerbates income inequality in Jamaica. Low-income households, which already struggle to meet their basic needs, are disproportionately affected by high electricity costs. These households often spend a significant portion of their income on energy, leaving less money for other essential goods and services such as food, healthcare, and education. As a result, energy poverty deepens existing social inequalities and impedes efforts to reduce poverty in the country.

Social Consequences

The social consequences of energy poverty in Jamaica are equally severe. Limited access to reliable and affordable energy services affects various aspects of daily life, including education, healthcare, and overall quality of life. In rural areas, where electricity access is often limited or unreliable, children are particularly disadvantaged. Without adequate lighting, students are unable to study effectively in the evenings, leading to lower educational outcomes and reduced opportunities for upward social mobility. Moreover, energy poverty contributes to poor healthcare outcomes in Jamaica. Many healthcare facilities, especially in rural areas, lack consistent access to electricity, which is essential for the operation of medical equipment, refrigeration of vaccines, and lighting.

This lack of reliable energy can lead to inadequate healthcare services, putting the lives of patients at risk and exacerbating public health challenges. Energy poverty also has a significant impact on gender equality in Jamaica. Women, who are typically responsible for household chores and caregiving, bear the brunt of energy poverty. They are often forced to spend long hours gathering firewood or other traditional fuels for cooking, which limits their time for education, income-generating activities, and participation in community life. This not only reinforces traditional gender roles but also perpetuates the cycle of poverty among women and girls.

Environmental Consequences

Energy poverty in Jamaica also has considerable environmental consequences. Due to the high cost and limited availability of modern energy services, many households rely on traditional biomass fuels such as wood and charcoal for cooking and heating. The widespread use of these fuels contributes to deforestation, soil degradation, and loss of biodiversity, which are critical environmental challenges in Jamaica. Dubbed the "land of wood and water", and home to over 300 endemic species of trees, Jamaica, sadly, is now only 30% (336,000 hectares) forested lands. The rate of deforestation is about 350 hectares per year (Planning Institute of Jamaica, 2009).

Moreover, the burning of biomass fuels releases harmful pollutants into the air, contributing to indoor and outdoor air pollution and exacerbating respiratory illnesses among the population.

Furthermore, Jamaica's reliance on imported fossil fuels for electricity generation not only drives up energy costs but also contributes to the country's carbon footprint. As a small island developing state, Jamaica is particularly vulnerable to the impacts of climate change, including rising sea levels, more frequent and intense hurricanes, and changing weather patterns. Energy poverty, therefore, not only harms the environment directly but also undermines the country's efforts to mitigate and adapt to climate change.

HEALTH CONSEQUENCES

The health consequences of energy poverty in Jamaica are closely linked to its social and environmental impacts. The use of traditional biomass fuels for cooking, often in poorly ventilated spaces, exposes households to high levels of indoor air pollution. This exposure is a leading cause of respiratory diseases, including chronic obstructive pulmonary disease (COPD) and acute respiratory infections, particularly among women and children. The World Health Organization (WHO) has identified indoor air pollution as a significant public health issue in developing countries, and Jamaica is no exception. All Jamaican locations being monitored for PM2.5, an air pollutant, have exceeded the WHO's 5 micrograms per cubic meter standard, according to preliminary studies conducted by the National Environment and Planning Agency (NEPA).

From Montego Bay to Mandeville to Kingston, air quality breaches global health standard (Murphy, 2022), this is mainly attributed to the fact that these areas are densely populated with factories, high rising buildings, and a lot of deforestation. In addition to respiratory illnesses, energy poverty can lead to malnutrition and food insecurity. Without reliable electricity, many households lack access to refrigeration, which is essential for preserving food and preventing spoilage. This can lead to a reliance on non-perishable, often less nutritious, foods, contributing to poor dietary outcomes and increased rates of malnutrition, particularly among children and the elderly.

Dr. Christopher Tufton, the Minister of Health in 2016, said that Jamaica has a high worldwide obesity risk, and that the country's annual weight gain is four times more than that of Americans and Nigerians. He added that programmes to address unhealthy eating in the nation will continue to be implemented by the government in collaboration with organizations like the Jamaica Association of Professionals in Nutrition and Dietetics (JAPINAD) (Hodges, 2016).

Energy poverty in Jamaica is a complex and multifaceted issue with far-reaching consequences for the country's economy, society, environment, and public health. The high cost of energy, coupled with limited access to reliable electricity, exacerbates income inequality, hinders economic growth, and perpetuates social disparities. It also contributes to environmental degradation and undermines efforts to address climate change, while posing significant health risks to the population.

Addressing energy poverty in Jamaica requires a concerted effort from the government, private sector, and international partners to increase access to affordable and sustainable energy services. This includes investing in renewable energy sources, improving energy efficiency, and expanding electricity infrastructure, particularly in rural areas. By tackling energy poverty, Jamaica can not only improve the quality of life for its citizens but also support sustainable development and build resilience to the challenges of the twenty-first century.

The Impact of Energy Poverty on Youth, Disabled, and Minority Groups

Energy poverty, defined as the lack of access to modern, reliable, and affordable energy services, is a pervasive issue that disproportionately affects vulnerable populations (Samarakoon, 2019). Among those most impacted are youth, disabled individuals, and minority groups, who face unique challenges in their daily lives due to limited access to energy. Approximately 1 billion people worldwide, or 13% of the world's population, do not have access to electricity, primarily in South Asia and Africa, according to the 2018 IEA World Energy Outlook. It is estimated that 600 million people, or 57% of the population, in sub-Saharan Africa do not have access to electricity, compared to 350 million people, or 9% of the population, in developing Asia. The attainment of universal energy access by 2030 was listed as one of the goals of the UN Agenda for Sustainable Development.

The consequences of energy poverty for these groups are profound, spanning economic, social, educational, and health dimensions. Understanding and addressing the specific impacts of energy poverty on these populations is essential for creating a more inclusive and equitable society.

Impact on Young Women

Energy poverty also affects the physical and mental well-being of youth. Without adequate heating or cooling, young people are exposed to extreme temperatures that can impact their health and overall comfort. Moreover, energy poverty can exacerbate feelings of social exclusion, as youth in energy-poor households may be unable to participate in social or extracurricular activities that require electricity, such as watching television, using social media, or charging mobile phones.

For instance, approximately 80% of elementary schools in Burkina Faso, Cameroon, Malawi, and Niger are without power (Knoth, 2015). Instead of going to school, getting ready for a test, or finishing their schoolwork, kids are sometimes made to gather firewood or clean drinking water for cooking, heating, and drinking. Firewood needs are reduced or eliminated by using other fuel sources or appliances, such as more efficient smoke hoods for cooking. Families can readily obtain drinking water thanks to solar-powered water pumps, which also lower the incidence of diarrhoea and other water-borne ailments that worsen sickness and low school attendance rates.

Furthermore, energy poverty can lead to intergenerational cycles of poverty. When young people are unable to complete their education due to energy-related challenges, they are less likely to secure stable, well-paying jobs in the future. This lack of economic opportunity can perpetuate poverty within families and communities, making it difficult for future generations to break free from the constraints of energy poverty.

Impact on Disabled Women

Disabled individuals face unique challenges related to energy poverty, as they often rely on energy-dependent medical devices, mobility aids, and other technologies to maintain their health and independence. For those who require equipment such as electric wheelchairs, ventilators, or home oxygen systems, a lack of reliable electricity can be life-threatening. Even short-term power outages can have serious consequences, leaving disabled individuals without the necessary support to manage their conditions.

Energy poverty also exacerbates the physical and social isolation experienced by many disabled individuals. Without access to transportation, communication technologies, or proper heating and cooling, disabled people may be confined to their homes, limiting their ability to engage with their communities, access healthcare, or participate in the workforce. This isolation can lead to increased rates of depression, anxiety, and other mental health issues, further compounding the challenges faced by disabled individuals in energy-poor households.

In addition to health and social impacts, energy poverty can strain the financial resources of disabled individuals and their families. The cost of operating energy-intensive medical equipment, combined with high electricity prices, can place a significant financial burden on households already struggling with medical expenses. This financial strain often forces disabled individuals and their families to make difficult choices between energy, healthcare, and other essential needs, leading to a lower quality of life and increased vulnerability.

IMPACT ON MINORITY GROUPS

Minority groups, including racial, ethnic, and indigenous communities, are disproportionately affected by energy poverty due to systemic inequalities and historical marginalization. These groups are more likely to live in energy-poor areas, such as rural regions or under-resourced urban neighbourhoods, where access to reliable and affordable energy is limited. The impact of energy poverty on minority groups is multifaceted, affecting their economic opportunities, health, and social inclusion. Energy poverty is generally associated with being at home more (due to unemployment, retirement, and caring responsibilities) and being involved in caring or domestic roles (Petrova & Simcock, 2021; Robinson, 2019; Sánchez-Guevara Sánchez et al., 2020; Anderson et al., 2012). It implies that gender has a role in energy poverty.

Economically, energy poverty exacerbates the existing disparities faced by minority groups. High energy costs consume a significant portion of household income, leaving less money for other necessities such as food, education, and healthcare. This financial strain can lead to higher rates of poverty and unemployment among minority populations, reinforcing the cycle of disadvantage.

Health outcomes are also negatively impacted by energy poverty within minority communities. The reliance on traditional biomass fuels for cooking and heating, often due to a lack of access to modern energy sources, contributes to indoor air pollution and associated respiratory illnesses (Jessel et al., 2019). Minority groups are also more likely to live in substandard housing that lacks proper insulation, heating, or cooling, further increasing their exposure to extreme temperatures and related health risks.

Socially, energy poverty contributes to the marginalization of minority groups by limiting their access to modern technologies and services that are essential for full participation in society. For example, limited access to the internet and digital communication tools can hinder educational and employment opportunities, making it difficult for minority individuals to access information, apply for jobs, or engage with broader societal networks. This digital divide reinforces social exclusion and limits the potential for upward mobility within these communities.

The impact of energy poverty on youth, disabled individuals, and minority groups is profound and multifaceted, affecting every aspect of their lives, from education and health to economic opportunities and social inclusion. Addressing energy poverty within these vulnerable populations requires targeted interventions that recognize and address the unique challenges they face. This includes investing in renewable energy infrastructure, expanding access to affordable and reliable energy services, and implementing policies that prioritize the needs of marginalized communities.

By addressing the specific impacts of energy poverty on these groups, policymakers can help create a more equitable society where all individuals, regardless of their background or circumstances, have access to the energy services they need to lead healthy, productive, and fulfilling lives. Tackling energy poverty is not only a matter of social justice but also a critical step towards achieving broader goals of sustainable development and inclusive growth.

REFERENCES

Adisa, P. O. (2020, December 11). *Let us end gender-based violence.* The Gleaner. https://jamaica-gleaner.com/article/commentary/20201211/opal-palmer-adisa-let-usend-gender-based-violence

Anderson, W., White, V., & Finney, A. D. (2012). Coping with low incomes and cold homes. *Energy Policy, 49,* 40–52. https://doi.org/10.1016/j.enpol.2012.01.002

Askwbcaribbean: Talking energy, finding solutions. (2022, October 22). *World Bank.* https://www.worldbank.org/en/events/2022/10/11/caribbean-talking-energy-finding-solutions#:~:text=of%20Biomass%2FWTE.-,With%20the%20global%20oil%20prices%20on%20the%20rise%2C%20the%20already,easing%20in%202023%20and%202024

Bennett Marsh, E. (2022, March 6). *OUR provides regulatory balance.* The Gleaner. https://jamaica-gleaner.com/article/commentary/20220306/elizabeth-bennett-marsh-ourprovides-regulatory-balance

BENNETT Senior business reporter bennettk@jamaicaobserver.com, K. (2024, March 27). *Dismantle JPS monopoly.* Jamaica Observer. https://www.jamaicaobserver.com/2024/03/27/dismantle-jps-monopoly/

Beuermann, D. W., et al. (2023). *Title of the work.* Publisher.

Beuermann, D. W., et al. (2024). *Title of the work.* Publisher.

Bryan, G. A. (2023, February 8). Women-led entrepreneurship in Jamaica: The dynamics between education and work. *UN Women Caribbean*. https://caribbean.unwomen.org/en/stories/press-release/2022/12/afro-descendant-women-entrepreneurs-benefit-from-business-development-bootcamp-in-jamaica

Cao, C., Duan, H., & Ng, L. L. (2023). The impact of gender inequality in higher education on female employment. *Journal of Education, Humanities and Social Sciences (EPHHR)*, *8*, 2355.

Children's Bureau. (2023). *A father's impact on child development*. https://calendar-dffcdads.org/fathers-impact-on-child-development/calendar-dffcdads.org

Douglas, B., & Hussain, S. (2018). *Measuring the Benefits of Energy Access: A Handbook for Development Practitioners*. https://doi.org/10.18235/0001459.

Duncan-Price, I., Merusi, S., & Haarr, R. (2021). *Gender-responsive socioeconomic study on the impact of COVID-19 on women in business and women entrepreneurs in Jamaica*. UN Women Caribbean. https://caribbean.unwomen.org/en/materials/publications/2021/7/gender-responsive-socioeconomic-study-on-the-impact-of-covid-19-onbusinesswomen-in-jamaica_caribbean

Evans, H. L. (1999). Gender and Achievement in Secondary Education in Jamaica: Kingston Policy Development Unit.

Gould, E., Schieder, J., & Geier, K. (2016, October 20). *What is the gender pay gap and is it real?* The complete guide to how women are paid less than men and why it can't be explained away. Economic Policy Institute. https://www.epi.org/publication/what-is-the-gender-pay-gap-and-is-it-real/

Guevara, Z., Mendoza-Tinoco, D., & Silva, D. (2023). The theoretical peculiarities of energy poverty research: A systematic literature review. *Energy Research & Social Science*, *105*, 103274. https://doi.org/10.1016/j.erss.2023.103274

Headly, J. (2021). *Title of the work*. Publisher.

Hedges, S. B., Cohen, W. B., Timyan, J., & Yang, Z. (2018). Haiti's biodiversity threatened by nearly complete loss of primary forest. *Proceedings of the National Academy of Sciences of the United States of America*, *115*(46), 11850–11855. https://doi.org/10.1073/pnas.1809753115

Hirsh, R. & Koomey, J. (2015). Electricity Consumption and Economic Growth: A New Relationship with Significant Consequences?. *The Electricity Journal*. *28*. https://doi.org/10.1016/j.tej.2015.10.002.

Hodges, P.-G. (2016, June 17). *Jamaica Information Service – the voice of Jamaica*. Health Ministry Supports Fight Against Unhealthy Eating. https://jis.gov.jm/

Hoominfar, E. (2021). Gender socialization. In W. Leal Filho, A. M. Azul, L. Brandli, P. G. Özuyar, & T. Wall (Eds.), *Gender equality: Encyclopedia of the UN Sustainable Development Goals* (pp. 1–10). Springer. https://doi.org/10.1007/978-3-319-95687-9_13

IDB Invest. (2022). Sustainability report 2022. *Inter-American Investment Corporation*. https://idbinvest.org/en/sustainability/sustainability_report_2022

Institute of Medicine and National Research Council. (2015). *Transforming the workforce for children birth through age 8: A unifying foundation*. The National Academies Press.

International Labour Organization. (2018). *Greening with jobs: World Employment Social Outlook 2018*. ILO.

Jagoe, K., Rossanese, M., Charron, D., Rouse, J., Waweru, F., Waruguru, M., Delapena, S., Piedrahita, R., Livingston, K., & Ipe, J. (2020). Sharing the burden: Shifts in family time use, agency and gender dynamics after introduction of new cookstoves in rural Kenya. *Energy Research & Social Science*, 64, 101413. https://doi.org/10.1016/j.erss.2019.101413

Jessel, S., Sawyer, S., & Hernández, D. (2019). Energy, poverty, and health in climate change: A comprehensive review of an emerging literature. *Frontiers in Public Health*, 7, 357. https://doi.org/10.3389/fpubh.2019.00357

Knoth, G. (2015, July 9). *A classroom's worst nightmare? Energy poverty*. ONE.org US. https://www.one.org/us/stories/a-classrooms-worst-nightmare-energy-poverty/

Lindwall, C. (2022). *What are the effects of climate change?*. Effects of Climate Change - Impacts and Examples. https://www.nrdc.org/stories/what-are-effects-climate-change

Maertens, L., & Stork, A. (2017, October 9). *The real story of Haiti's forests*. Books & ideas. https://booksandideas.net/The-Real-Story-of-Haiti-s-Forests

Marsh, J. (2023, May 22). *The state of renewable energy in Jamaica*. The Borgen Project. https://borgenproject.org/renewable-energy-in-jamaica/

McKenzie, V. (2023, November 27). *Jamaica to go nuclear in bid to lower costs, end energy poverty - our Today*. Our Today -. https://our.today/jamaica-to-go-nuclear-in-bid-to-lower-costs-end-energy-poverty/

Mohammed, G. F., & Hashish, R. K. H. (2015). Sexual violence against females and its impact on their sexual function. Egyptian *Journal of Forensic Sciences*, 5(3), 96–102. https://doi.org/10.1016/j.ejfs.2014.08.004

Mokate, K. M. (Ed.). (2004). *Women's participation in social development: Experiences from Asia, Latin America, and the Caribbean*. Inter-American Development Bank. https://doi.org/10.18235/0012299

Murphy, J. (2022, April 26). *Pollution danger*. Lead Stories | Jamaica Gleaner. https://jamaica-gleaner.com/article/lead-stories/20220426/pollution-danger

Nyandoro, M. (2024). Water in Botswana: Selective distribution of a finite commodity among indigenes (San), African villages and non-indigenous white minority communities, 1880s–2020. *The Dyke*, 17(2), Article 8. https://doi.org/10.10520/ejc-dyke_v17_n2_a8

Petrova, S., & Simcock, N. (2021). Gender and energy: Domestic inequities reconsidered. *Social and Cultural Geography*, 22(6), 849–867. https://doi.org/10.1080/14649365.2019.1645200

Planning Institute of Jamaica. (2009, June). *Natural resources and environmental management sector plan*. Vision 2030 Jamaica. https://www.vision2030.gov.jm/wpcontent/uploads/sites/2/2020/12/Microsoft-Word-Natural-Resources-and-Environmental-Managment-June-2009.pdf

Policy Planning Development and Evaluation Division, Research Unit. (2018). *Title of the work*. Ministry of Science, Energy, Telecommunications and Transport. mset.gov.jm

Robinson, C. (2019). Energy poverty and gender in England: A spatial perspective. *Geoforum*, 104, 222–233. https://doi.org/10.1016/j.geoforum.2019.05.001

Samarakoon, S. (2019). 'A justice and wellbeing centered framework for analysing energy poverty in the Global South'. *Ecological Economics*, 165, p. 106385. https://doi.org/10.1016/J.ECOLECON.2019.106385

Sánchez-Guevara Sánchez, C., Sanz Fernández, A., & Núñez Peiró, M. (2020). Feminisation of energy poverty in the city of Madrid. *Energy and Buildings*, 223, 110157. https://doi.org/10.1016/j.enbuild.2019.110157

Saner, R., & Yiu, L. (2019). Jamaica's development of women entrepreneurship: Challenges and opportunities. *Public Administration and Policy: An Asia-Pacific Journal*, 22(2), 152–172. https://doi.org/10.1108/PAP-09-2019-0023

Smelser, N. J., & Baltes, P. B. (Eds.). (2001). *International encyclopedia of the social & behavioral sciences*. Elsevier.

Statistical Institute of Jamaica, Inter-American Development Bank, & UN Women. (2018). *Women's Health Survey 2016: Jamaica—Summary Report*. https://caribbean.unwomen.org/sites/default/files/Field%20Office%20Caribbean/Attachments/Publications/2018/20181012%20AF%20Jamaica%20Summary%20for%20digital.pdf

The Gleaner. (2014, December 1). *Women continue to head most Jamaican families with children*. https://jamaica-gleaner.com/power/56947JamaicaGleaner

The Gleaner. (2023). *JPS makes record profit from summer*. https://jamaica-gleaner.com/article/business/20230915/jps-makes-record-profit-summer

UNICEF. (2007). *The state of the world's children 2007: Women and children—the double dividend of gender equality*. https://www.unicef.org/reports/state-worlds-children-2007

U.S. Agency for International Development. (2017). *USAID report to Congress on health-related research and development for fiscal year 2017*. https://www.usaid.gov/document/usaid-report-congress-health-related-research-and-development-fiscal-year-2017USAID

Watson Williams, C. (2018). *Jamaica women's health survey 2016: Final report.* Inter-American Development Bank & UN Women. https://doi.org/10.18235/0001170

World Bank Group. (2024). *Results and performance of the World Bank Group 2024: Managing results in an uncertain world.* https://documents.worldbank.org/en/publication/documents-reports/documentdetail/099841003072529467/secbos11faeefa037180061e7fc55ee14ed World Bank

World Health Organization. (2024, May 7). *WHO Results Report 2023 shows notable health achievements and calls for concerted drive toward Sustainable Development Goals.* https://www.who.int/news/item/07-05-2024-who-results-report-2023-shows-notable-health-achievements-and-calls-for-concerted-drive-toward-sustainable-development-goals

CHAPTER 6

Recommendations

Abstract This chapter provides a concise summary and recommendations for the measures to guarantee that we have more efficient energy sources, particularly for women who live in low-income homes. It also speaks to the importance of transitioning to renewable energy and its implications for a developing country like Jamaica. The study focuses on seven areas that the author established in forming recommendations to assist women in these low-income households. These include legislation, regulatory, policies, institutional, financial and technical, which are key for both providers and suppliers of renewable energy. In addition, there is a need for better education, and the best way to achieve this is through recommendations. This chapter also investigates the role of key stakeholders in managing clean energy sources. It also gives a quick overview of the implications if each stakeholder is a part of the discussion.

Keywords Legislation • Policies • Regulatory • Institution and stakeholders

Recommendation to Improve Smarter Energy Sources

This chapter provides a concise summary of the measures that must be taken to guarantee that we have more intelligent and efficient energy sources, particularly for women who live in low-income homes. For Jamaica to get clean energy, we must keep in mind that the nation's dedication to sustainability is fuelled by several elements.

Affordable, contemporary energy should be available to all citizens, as this affects household consumption and livelihoods, production techniques, and overall environmental protection. As a result, how countries approach the issues of energy production and distribution has broad implications that necessitate a plan that considers the numerous impacting factors. Jamaica's small open economy depends mostly on imported fossil fuels for energy use, manufacturing, and transportation. Less domestic energy security follows, driving up the price of goods and services and contributing to an increase in pollutant emissions. Nearly everyone now has access to power because of the government's response to the energy sector, and the energy mix is diversifying with an increase in alternative and renewable sources.

Like many other countries, Jamaica must overcome the obstacle of switching to more intelligent and sustainable energy sources to fight climate change, save energy prices, and guarantee long-term energy security. It is essential to consider important areas including financial incentives, regulation and standards, technology and innovation, and education and awareness to accomplish these aims. To encourage more intelligent and sustainable energy sources in Jamaica, this essay examines the key suggestions in each of these categories. This study will examine the suggestions derived from Barbados, since Jamaica may connect to them from a regionalism standpoint due to their common historical background. Every topic will be emphasized and thoroughly examined, along with suggestions and illustrations that might lessen danger factors.

Jamaica should seek to minimize prices, increase efficiency, and lessen its environmental impact by regulating the energy sector to allow for more producers and cleaner sources. Like other island nations, Barbados has historically relied heavily on imported fossil fuels to meet its energy needs (Marshall & Koon, 2021). However, the island has started to make a significant shift towards renewable energy sources in response to growing fuel prices, worries about energy security, and the escalating global climate problem. "Hats off to Mia Mottley, 57" for leading the initiative as in

2019, her unwavering commitment to make Barbados fossil fuel-free by 2030. Mottley has become a global leader in the fight for equitable access to the resources that countries require to tackle climate change (Robertson, 2023). Since taking office as prime minister in 2018, Mottley's remarks at the UN General Assembly have garnered her attention on a global scale.

We must first investigate Jamaica's current level of energy reliance before we can offer recommendations for the various sectors of renewable energy in the country. The majority of Jamaica's energy demands are met by fossil fuels, mostly oil. Approximately 89% of energy comes from these sources, with renewables accounting for 11% and solar energy contributing just 1%. Because it imports the bulk of its oil, Jamaica is affected by growing expenses. The price of imported oil exceeded the proceeds from exports by nearly 118% in 2010. Thus, relying only on fossil fuels is not sustainable for the country's ecosystem or economy (Marsh, 2023).

Many Jamaicans pay a high premium to power their homes and businesses to offset the expense of garbage and imports. Because of the unpredictability of oil prices, people who depend on it sometimes find themselves in severe financial situations. Out of 82 low-to-middle-income countries with high rates of energy poverty, Jamaica gets the highest score due to a lack of appropriate energy infrastructure. While most of Jamaica's energy is now produced by fossil fuels, recent events suggest that this may not always be the case. Numerous organizations have already made steps to expand the usage of renewable energy sources. For example, the Jamaica Energy Security and Efficiency Enhancement Project cut the nation's dependency on oil by 24% in just seven years.

In 2020, the Ministry of Education, Youth, and Information made mention of investing $60 million on alternative energy (solar energy from photovoltaic systems) during the 2020/2021 fiscal year to cut power costs at government-owned schools around the island (Morris, 2020). For this fund has been allocated in the 2020/2021 estimates of expenditure, now before the House of Representatives. This implementation will take place through the Solar Energy Projects and supervised by the National Education Trust Limited.

To reduce electricity costs at government-owned schools around the island, the Ministry of Education, Youth, and Information announced in 2020 that it will spend $60 million on alternative energy (solar energy from photovoltaic systems) for the 2020–2021 budget year (MOE spent $60 million on solar energy in schools, 2020). The 2020–2021 spending estimates that are now before the House of Representatives include funding for this fund. This implementation will be overseen by the National Education Trust Limited and carried out through the Solar Energy Projects. This is mostly being done to reduce costs. The Solar Energy Projects aim to lower current power expenses at participating schools by 40–70% and supply alternative energy/solar energy using photovoltaic systems, hence reducing dependency on the Jamaica Public Service Co. Limited. Morris (2020) states that the National Education Trust Limited will oversee managing the Solar Energy Projects' execution. Before entering the Public-Private Partnership's Transitional Stage, the government will undertake structural repairs, upgrades, and retrofitting of the roofs of the chosen schools.

During the 2019/2020 fiscal year, the government performed an energy audit and structural examination of roofs, hired a project advisor and a transaction adviser, created a business case, and began rehabilitation work at several schools considered in need of repairs. The primary physical goal of the initiative is to install solar systems in 30 secondary schools. Kumar (2020) argues that while traditional energy sources like coal, gas, and oil are very helpful to a nation's economy, their detrimental effects on the environment have made us use them sparingly and have caused us to turn our attention to renewable energy sources. Using renewable energy sources can help prevent problems related to the environment, society, and economy because they are thought to be environmentally friendly and release few or no pollutants and dangerous gases like sulphur dioxide, carbon dioxide, and so forth (Kumar, 2020). Since renewable resources may be recycled to produce useful energy, Kumar (2020) predicted that they will become a significant source of power generation soon.

According to popular belief, wind power generation is thought to have the most positive social consequences, utilize the least amount of water, and produce the fewest greenhouse gas emissions. After geothermal, solar, and hydropower, it is thought to be one of the greenest renewable energy sources. As clean energy resources, these resources can help reduce greenhouse gas emissions and global warming (US Energy Information Administration, 2022). The appropriate use of renewable energy systems can result in local employment, improved health, job opportunities, job creation, consumer choice, life standard improvement, social bond formation, income development, demographic impacts, social bond building, and community development. Along with the outstanding benefits of these resources, some drawbacks exist, such as the variation of output due to seasonal change, which is common for wind and hydroelectric power plants; thus, special design and consideration are required, which are fulfilled by the hardware and software as computer technology advances.

In the backdrop of a considerable global increase in energy consumption, primarily due to rising living standards in developing and emerging countries, renewable energy helps to address growing concerns about future energy pricing and energy security (World Economic Forum, 2022). It is recommended to focus on renewable energy solutions, as many are already market competitive. Decentralized power generation can effectively attract small-scale private investments, and expanding the renewable energy sector has the potential to create numerous job opportunities—a key public policy priority for many countries. Investing in renewable energy not only supports project development, construction, and installation but also fosters small-scale private investment.

According to the Asian Infrastructure Investment Bank (2021), the renewable energy value chain consists of four key components: equipment manufacturing and distribution, project development, construction and installation, and operations and maintenance. Employment trends in the manufacturing and distribution of renewable energy technologies are like those seen in other capital goods industries. However, employment patterns in project development and construction differ significantly, as these jobs are project-based, and job stability relies on a steady stream of projects. In contrast, employment in operations and maintenance tends to be more stable. When a major new installation is commissioned, total employment tends to expand in spurts. According to the International Energy Summary, globally, most sections of the renewable energy sector are still in the early phases of development and are developing fast in relation to their existing low base (with a reasonably big installed base, hydropower is an exception).

The trend varies significantly when viewed in the context of national labour markets. For each major technology, some countries show minimal activity (Haiti, Chad, and Yemen), others experience rapid growth (Uruguay, Denmark, and Lithuania), some see moderate capacity expansion (European Union), while others have a more established sector. Challenges with skills and labour shortages or surpluses in renewable energy often arise when activity accelerates quickly, leading to a sharp increase in labour demand, and later, when the pace of new installations either rapidly increases or decreases. These skill shortages are expected to be less severe in developed countries with a highly skilled workforce. In contrast, most developing countries face greater difficulties due to the lack of high-quality training and education providers, making it harder to address growing skill shortages.

In Jamaica, several organizations are working to increase renewable energy in order to lessen energy poverty. For example, the founders of Radiant Energy Ltd believe that more sustainable energy might help Jamaica's economy. The business provides clean power at a lower cost than fossil fuels because rising costs impede economic growth and worsen poverty.

But according to Philipp (2023), Jamaica—known for its vibrant culture and stunning beaches—is currently experiencing a serious energy crisis that will influence the country's population as well as its economy. Because the island nation's energy needs are mostly met by fossil fuels—oil in particular—it is susceptible to price increases and negative environmental effects. Jamaicans find it difficult to afford the hefty energy costs and trash fees associated with running their homes and businesses. Despite these obstacles, hints of improvement are appearing as renewable energy efforts gain traction.

And the situation of renewable energy in Jamaica looks to be influencing the country's poverty. One of the main goals in creating a "new Jamaica" is to fully utilize renewable energy sources for the nation's energy sector, according to Hon. Daryl Vaz, Minister of Science, Energy, and Technology. "The expected outcome will lead to decreased susceptibility to external economic shocks, increased resilience against the adverse consequences of geopolitical tensions, decreased energy costs, complete access to electricity, and a decrease in the nation's carbon footprint," the prime minister declared (William, 2021).

By 2030, Jamaica wants to generate 33% of its electricity from renewable sources, and by 2037, 50%. Office of the Prime Minister, Jamaica (2023) projects that by 2025, about 22% of Jamaica's electricity will come from renewable sources. He said that the Cabinet established a board for the entity in charge of obtaining more power production capacity in accordance with the power Act 2015 to ensure that the nation's energy goals are met. Furthermore, he announced that the Ministry will carry out an energy end-use survey to examine modifications in electrical load patterns and end-use consumption allocations, as well as a renewable energy penetration study to update and validate the degree of renewable energy adoption.

The transition to a renewable energy future in Jamaica necessitates effective oversight, regulation, and collaboration among government agencies, private sector entities, and international stakeholders. The Jamaican government has made notable strides in establishing a policy framework for renewable energy development. Key documents such as the National Energy Policy and the Integrated Resource Plan outline specific targets for increasing renewable energy usage, enhancing energy efficiency, and reducing emissions.

The Ministry of Science, Energy, and Technology (MSET) is pivotal in overseeing the energy transition. It ensures that renewable energy projects adhere to national standards while contributing to broader development objectives. Additionally, organizations like Jamaica Energy Partners (JEP) and the Electricity Sector Enterprise Team (ESET) are instrumental in shaping strategic decisions and steering the future direction of the energy sector.

- Accelerating the expansion of the renewable energy system and enhancing its resilience are essential. This entails investing heavily in energy storage technology development, smart grid implementation, and system modernization. In order to increase the share of renewable energy sources in the grid without jeopardizing its stability and dependability, several actions are essential.
- Second, to guarantee that women in rural communities have access to reasonably priced and dependable electricity, the government should invest more in off-grid energy options. Access to solar and wind energy could be increased through subsidies or other forms of financial assistance for individuals and small enterprises. Furthermore, creating microgrid systems that can function both independently and in tandem with the main grid will increase resilience and energy security in isolated communities.
- Third, it is imperative to improve the framework of regulations and policies. The private sector would spend more in renewable energy if the permission procedures were made simpler, bureaucratic barriers were reduced, and energy project approval procedures were made more transparent. Furthermore, encouraging public-private partnerships could successfully raise funds for energy projects that are off the grid as well as those that are connected to it.

According to Richards and Yabar (2022), energy generation plays a crucial role in a nation's development as it impacts the production and distribution of goods and services needed for the provision of social amenities. The modes of production, distribution, and consumption have a significant impact on other sectors of the economy, including tourism, agriculture, healthcare, and infrastructure development. Therefore, limiting petroleum imports is necessary for both energy security and long-term green growth. According to the World Integrated Trade Solution, oil imports made up 1.63 billion USD in 2018, representing 7–10% of Jamaica's GDP. The move away from fossil fuels gives the prospect of reallocating resources from spending on petroleum imports to growing human capital and developing new sectors. As a result, the revitalization of the sugar sector stands to profit from the reallocated monies.

On the other hand, due to the absence of fossil fuel sources, Jamaica currently imports most of its petroleum to meet its energy needs; 93% or more of people have access to electricity generated by petroleum. However, as oil imports make up 9–11% of the island's GDP, rising fuel consumption and a lack of funds to pay for an increasing oil bill limit energy security. Comparative cost analyses indicate that by 2030, Jamaica might save up to USD 12.5 billion on energy system costs. As a result, the negative environmental and economic consequences need a transition away from fossil fuels and towards other Renewable Energy solutions. In Jamaica, the percentage of renewable energy sources has climbed from 9% in 2009 to 20% now (Yabar et al., 2022).

Therefore, switching from fossil fuels to renewable energy has benefits that go beyond increased energy security. To fully utilize its energy resources, increase its worldwide competitiveness and energy security, and reduce its carbon footprint, Jamaica must develop renewable energy sources, according to the country's 2009 National Energy Policy. This is further emphasized by the policy's goal. The National Policy also establishes goals for the percentage of renewable energy in the mix of energy sources through 2030. According to the plan, by 2030, 20% of the country's energy would be from renewable sources. Two of the main objectives of setting these national targets for renewable energy are to reassure investors and to encourage continued development in technologies that can produce power from a variety of renewable sources (Ministry of Energy and Mining, 2010).

Examining centralized and decentralized sustainable energy systems is crucial to understanding their impact on mitigating energy poverty and advancing social justice. Decentralized renewable energy solutions, such as solar microgrids and community-based initiatives, offer significant benefits in Jamaica, particularly for low-income women who face compounded challenges related to energy access and affordability. Globally, decentralized power generation is emerging as a transformative approach, shifting reliance from centralized networks to localized energy production tailored to community needs.

According to the report *Decentralized Power Generation: Community Microgrids with Ocean Energy* (2024), decentralized systems can be customized to meet local requirements, reducing dependence on costly centralized networks and enabling communities to generate and manage their own energy. However, the success of such systems relies on ownership and governance models that prioritize energy justice, ensuring equitable access and decision-making.

This approach is especially relevant in Jamaica, where energy poverty—defined as a lack of access to modern energy services—disproportionately affects low-income women due to socio-economic inequalities. Decentralized renewable energy systems offer substantial social and economic advantages for low-income women. These systems guarantee dependable and economical energy availability, diminishing dependence on kerosene or wood, which are expensive, inefficient, and detrimental to health. Access to clean energy allows women to participate in income-generating activities, alleviating the time stress of home responsibilities and enhancing overall quality of life. Moreover, decentralized systems can incorporate women into governance and ownership frameworks, guaranteeing their active participation in decision-making and direct benefits from energy initiatives.

Decentralized solutions currently constitute a fundamental component of national electrification policies in an increasing number of countries experiencing significant access shortages, including Nigeria, Rwanda, and the United Republic of Tanzania (IRENA, 2022). Decentralized renewable energy sources have historically facilitated fundamental electricity access. In 2019, about 138 million individuals out of a total of 176 million benefitted from solar illumination solutions, which are classified below Tier 1 of the Multi-Tier Framework (see to Box 5). (International Energy Agency, International Renewable Energy Agency, United Nations Statistics Division, World Bank, and World Health Organization, 2019).

Energy justice underscores equitable access to energy resources, reasonable decision-making processes, and the consideration of the needs of marginalized communities. Decentralized renewable energy systems adhere to these objectives by prioritizing marginalized populations and empowering women through leadership and employment opportunities.

Cooperatives or community-led initiatives that engage women in the management of solar mini-grids or wind farms guarantee equitable distribution of energy development benefits. Tackling energy poverty among economically disadvantaged women aligns with overarching social justice objectives. According to Hughes (2018) access to energy enhances educational, healthcare, and economic prospects, directly confronting entrenched gender disparities.

Emphasizing decentralized renewable energy systems in Jamaica reveals a means to address energy disparities, empower economically disadvantaged women, and promote energy and social equity. By promoting localized, inclusive energy solutions that prioritize community engagement and fairness, Jamaica may establish a more sustainable and equitable energy future, while advancing broader objectives of poverty alleviation and gender equality.

The institutional framework outlines the key stakeholders in the renewable energy sector, as well as their roles and responsibilities. The goals, approaches, and steps necessary to make the policy easier to implement are described in the strategic framework, which serves as support for the policy framework. The five (5) objectives listed in the Strategic Framework supporting this policy will help in the following:

1. Creating economic, physical, and planning conditions for the sustainable development of Jamaica's renewable energy sources.
2. An enabling environment for the implementation of important policy tools (financial and fiscal) to promote renewable energy (by shifting national resources and investments to RETs).
3. A dynamic legal and regulatory environment that responds to the growth and development of renewable energy.
4. Improved technical competence and public knowledge of renewable energy through successful training programmes, information distribution tactics, and continued government communications.
5. Sustained R&D and innovation in existing and upcoming renewable energy technologies (Planning Institute of Jamaica, 2022).

The framework identifies the major entities in charge of achieving each goal and provides short-, medium-, and long-term strategic orientations for the public, commercial, and industrial sectors. Designed to be adaptive and flexible, the framework allows for the exploration of new opportunities as they arise. Jamaica is actively working to enhance the availability and affordability of electricity, exemplified by tax exemptions on wind turbines and solar panels. The country's ongoing transition to renewable energy suggests a promising future for both its economy and environment (Marsh, 2023). To successfully achieve these objectives, it is crucial to focus on areas such as Education and Awareness, Financial Incentives, Regulation and Standards, and Technology and Innovation. Implementing these recommendations could yield significant benefits.

Figure 6.1 highlights the fundamental connections between security, economic growth, and environmental protection, but these goals can only be realized through diligent efforts and the implementation of recommendations to enhance the competencies and sustainability of citizens. Clean and efficient energy use is crucial for sustainable development and tackling climate change. Although numerous technologies and practices exist to promote clean and efficient energy consumption, various obstacles

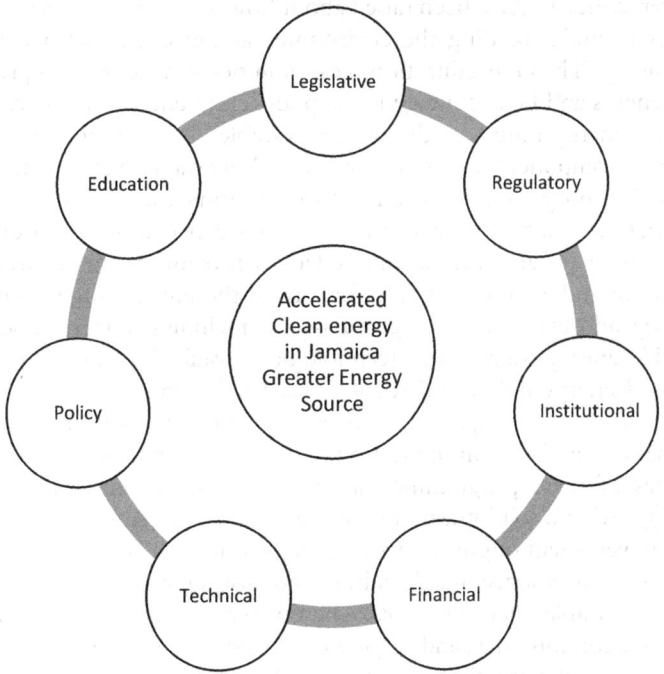

Fig. 6.1 Recommended areas to encourage clean energy

still hinder their adoption by individuals and organizations. In this chapter, we will examine recommendations and policies aimed at promoting clean and efficient energy use, supported by scholarly research and case studies.

EDUCATION AND AWARENESS

A key recommendation for promoting clean and efficient energy consumption is increasing education and awareness. Many people and organizations are unaware of the advantages of clean energy and, as a result, do not prioritize it in their decision-making. Education and awareness campaigns can address this issue by providing information on the benefits of clean and efficient energy use, along with practical tips for implementation (Pietrapertosa et al., 2021). Governments, organizations, and educational institutions all have a crucial role in raising public awareness about sustainable energy choices, as these decisions significantly impact the nation. However, concerns have been raised about how to effectively engage communities in understanding the environmental and economic benefits of clean energy. Through education, communities can better comprehend these benefits and be encouraged to support clean energy initiatives.

As the energy industry advances, renewable energy becomes a more important component of the energy mix. Renewable energy education and training programmes are critical for ensuring that the workforce is appropriately qualified to meet the industry's expectations (Frąckiewicz, 2023). These programmes are intended to provide graduates with the information and abilities required for jobs in the burgeoning energy sector. They address a wide range of issues, including energy efficiency, renewable energy sources and technologies, sustainable energy development, and energy policy and regulations. Participants learn how to discover, assess, and implement renewable energy solutions using a combination of classroom education and hands-on practice. As a result, graduates of these programmes are well-prepared to enter the energy industry, having a solid grasp of renewable energy systems.

The government ought to invest in public outreach and education programmes to foster a sustainable culture and raise awareness about the benefits of renewable energy sources. These projects should aim to educate businesses, communities, and schools on the benefits of renewable energy, its impact on climate change, and available technologies. Jamaica, like Ghana, has a wealth of untapped renewable resources that are ready for utilization. Jamaica has extensive renewable energy resources, notably solar, wind, and biomass, that have not been completely utilized in the past but have the potential to fulfil a major amount of the country's future energy needs. In 2004, alternative and indigenous energy sources including wood, bagasse, and hydropower contributed for 8% of Jamaica's overall energy supply (Loy & Coviello, 2005).

A key factor contributing to Jamaica's dependency on imported crude oil and petroleum products, which account for 90% of its energy requirements, is a lack of knowledge and awareness (Loy & Coviello, 2005). According to a 2005 report from the Ministry of Commerce, Science, and Technology titled "Renewable Energies Potential in Jamaica," approximately US$ 800 million was spent on importing crude oil and petroleum products in 2003, with the average cost of raw oil being US$ 28.4 per barrel and refined products costing US$ 30. According to project papers from the Economic Commission for Latin America and the Caribbean, Jamaica has the capacity to generate 16 barrels of renewable energy daily. However, as global oil prices rose in 2004, the cost of petroleum imports exceeded US$1.2 billion.

The government should integrate renewable energy education into the national curriculum at all levels. This will equip future generations with the knowledge to support and utilize renewable energy in their daily lives and careers. The Barbados National Energy Policy (BNEP) emphasizes education, awareness, and employment development in the energy industry. Barbados has launched new academic and vocational training programmes to support its objective of transitioning totally to renewable energy by 2030. The Ministry of Energy has also developed an online directory, the Smart Energy Educational Catalogue, which lists renewable energy courses from institutions like the Samuel Jackman Prescod Institute of Technology (SJPI) and the Barbados Vocational Training Board (BVTB).

Jamaica, facing similar historical challenges as Barbados, can adopt similar strategies and collaborations to ensure future sustainability. The Ministry of Science, Energy and Technology should support public-private partnerships with Barbados, the Samuel Jackman Prescod Institute of Technology (SJPI), or locally with the Human Employment and Resource Training Trust/National Training Agency (HEART TRUST/NTA). By partnering with private sector organizations to promote education and awareness, and by developing educational campaigns and seminars, Jamaica can effectively disseminate information about renewable energy and its applications, leveraging industry resources and expertise (Fig. 6.2).

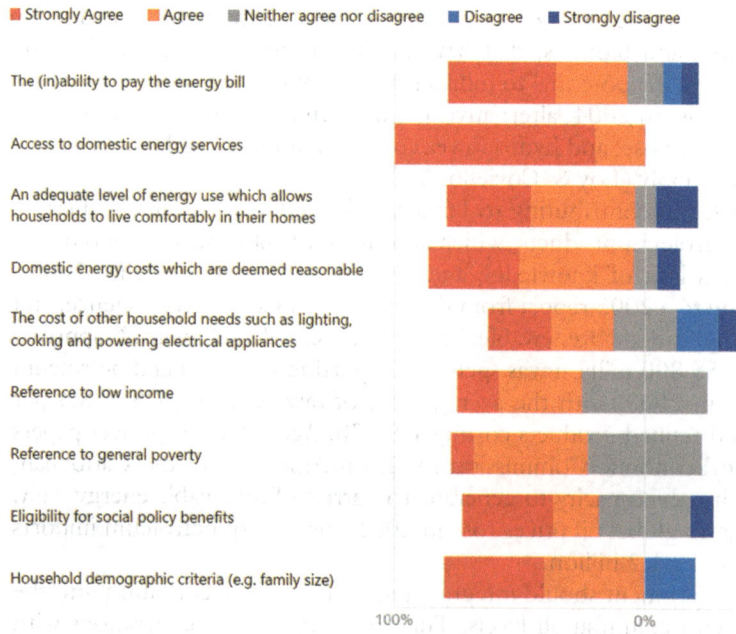

Fig. 6.2 Features suggested that should be part of a concept of energy poverty

The stacked bar graph above shows the respondents' opinion on different considerations that should be taken into account as it relates to energy poverty. Majority of respondents "agree" and "strongly agree" to the suggestion listed. Approximately 80% of the respondents strongly agree that more consideration should be taken into account for access to domestic energy services when it comes on to energy poverty. Respectively, majority of the respondents (approximately 40%) agree that more consideration should be taken into account for household demography (family size etc). However, 15% of the respondents neither agree nor disagree that "reference to general poverty" should be taken into account when it comes on to "energy poverty" in general, whilst approximately 40% of the respondents agree that "reference to general poverty" should be taken into account when it comes on to "energy poverty" in general.

The government should provide an enabling framework to support the development, dissemination, implementation, and transfer of existing, developing, and long-term cost-effective, cleaner, and more efficient technologies and practices in both the public and private sectors. Furthermore, government ministries, with the assistance of educational key partners such as USAID, can facilitate and promote research, development, and demonstrations of new energy technologies by enhancing institutional capacity, expanding R&D infrastructure, attracting and retaining quality expertise, and developing long-term funding mechanisms. Studies have shown that education and awareness campaigns can be effective in changing behaviour towards clean and efficient energy consumption. For example, a study in Mexico revealed that an educational campaign on energy conservation resulted in a 10% decrease in household electricity usage. Likewise, research in India showed that an awareness campaign about solar energy significantly boosted the number of households installing solar water heaters (Castellanos-Sosa et al., 2022).

Financial Incentives

Financial incentives are crucial for promoting clean and efficient energy use. Many individuals and organizations hesitate to invest in these technologies due to perceived high costs, despite their potential for long-term savings. Financial incentives can alleviate this issue by offering direct or indirect support for those investing in clean energy. Loans, grants, and tax credits are among examples. For example, in the United States, the federal government offers tax breaks for renewable energy projects such as solar panels and wind turbines. Similarly, Germany has a feed-in tariff system that ensures compensation to people who generate renewable energy.

According to the Jamaica Information Service (2015), in 2015, Hon. Phillip Paulwell, Minister of Science, Technology, Energy, and Mining, noted that the government's policy shift on alternative energy sources, including the introduction of incentives, has led to greater use and investment in renewable energy options. The policy provides low-interest loans to companies and families to purchase renewable energy equipment, particularly solar systems. According to McIntosh (2015), the government has adopted a number of policy measures to stimulate investment in renewable energy projects. This includes taking away the Petroleum Corporation of Jamaica's (PCJ) sole right to develop all renewable energy projects. Subsequently, the Office of Utilities Regulation (OUR) published a Request for Proposals to secure up to 115 megawatts of renewable energy. The policy involves low-interest loans to help companies and homeowners acquire renewable energy systems, mostly solar devices.

Despite having abundant natural resources, Jamaica's sustainable development is hindered by the high startup costs for harnessing these resources, as equipment is generally expensive and needs to be imported. To address this, the government could implement Power Purchase Agreements (PPAs) and Feed-in Tariffs. These mechanisms provide financial stability and incentivize investment in renewable energy projects by guaranteeing a fixed rate for energy producers. Blair-Loy (2005) suggests that the government should also consider financial and fiscal incentives, such as income tax rebates, GCT waivers, or reduced duty taxes, to lower the investment threshold for projects with high initial costs.

Furthermore, renewable electricity purchase rates should be determined based on projected avoided costs—considering the costs of displaced power plants—rather than relying solely on a least-cost principle. These rates should also include a bonus for environmental and social benefits. To be appealing to operators and financial institutions, tariffs should be fixed for at least ten years, with adjustments for annual inflation and currency devaluation. Additionally, the rates should ensure a reasonable return on investment without raising overall electricity generation costs and account for the rising costs of fossil fuels over the contract period.

Jamaica's unsustainable reliance on imported fossil fuels is a major driving force behind its transition to renewable energy. According to the World Bank, Jamaica imports more than 90% of its energy, rendering it subject to global oil price changes (Joseph, 2023). This reliance has resulted in some of the highest electricity costs in the Caribbean for both residential and business customers. To solve this issue, the government has established a goal of generating 50% of the country's power from renewable sources by 2030. One potential answer is the introduction of Green Bonds, which are intended to raise funding for renewable energy projects. These bonds can attract environmentally aware investors and serve as a long-term funding source for projects like solar farms, wind turbines, and energy storage facilities.

Regulation and Standards

Regulation and standards are another essential guideline for promoting clean and efficient energy usage. Governments may help promote clean and efficient energy usage by establishing laws and standards for energy efficiency and emissions reduction. These norms and standards may apply to both individual families and organizations, such as enterprises and industries. Regulations and standards include building codes, appliance requirements, and pollution standards. The European Union, for example, has rules that establish minimum energy performance criteria for buildings, appliances, and cars. Furthermore, European Union legislators have established a deadline for the sale of new autos using combustion engines. They passed legislation on Tuesday that basically bans automobiles with gasoline or diesel engines from being sold at dealerships beginning in 2035 (Eddy, 2023).

This is to promote more renewable form of energy usage and natural energy invention. Another example, in China the chief economic planning body of the nation declared that this year, 70 national standards pertaining to energy efficiency, carbon capture technologies, and carbon footprints will be established. The purpose of these new regulations is to give Chinese companies and industries a precise framework for measuring and lowering their carbon emissions. Furthermore, by 2025, China wants to have 100 pilot projects in place for the control of carbon emissions. The country's larger plan to reach peak carbon emissions and eventually achieve carbon neutrality includes these projects as essential elements (George, 2024).

According to CARICOM (2020), energy is inextricably related to the production of commodities and the delivery of services within the Caribbean Community. Economic expansion and social development are often accompanied by rising energy demand, and greater access to modern energy, particularly electricity, has helped enterprises while also improving the quality of life for many people in the area. Over the last three years, CARICOM has been developing a Regional Energy saving Strategy to capitalize on the region's substantial, yet mostly untapped, energy saving potential.

The area has addressed the Strategy by developing codes and standards through the CARICOM Secretariat; the Regional Institutions in charge of standards and energy, namely the CARICOM Regional Organization for Standards and Quality (CROSQ) and the Caribbean Centre for Renewable Energy and Energy Efficiency (CCREEE); and the Member States through their own government ministries and national standards bodies. The area has advanced the Strategy by developing standards and regulations with the assistance of the CARICOM Secretariat, the CARICOM Regional Organization for Standards and Quality (CROSQ), the Caribbean Centre for Renewable Energy and Energy Efficiency (CCREEE), and individual Member States' government ministries and national standards bodies.

The Jamaican government has actively promoted the expansion of renewable energy through various legislation and programmes. Recent attempts include the adoption of a net billing plan, which allows consumers who produce their own energy from renewable sources to sell surplus power back into the grid (Joseph, 2023). As component of the Vision 2030 Jamaica—National Development Plan and the Sustainable Development Goals (SDGs), national outcome 10 focuses on energy security and efficiency, defining many strategies and actions required to meet renewable energy and power access targets. These programmes focus on expanding energy sources while also improving efficiency and conservation (Planning Institute of Jamaica, 2022). As a proposal, the government should introduce Renewable Portfolio Standards (RPS). Create Renewable Portfolio Standards that mandate a particular percentage of power from renewable sources in the national energy mix. This legal framework creates a market for renewable energy while maintaining steady demand.

The Barbados National Energy Policy (BNEP) aims to achieve 100% renewable energy and carbon neutrality by 2030. It builds on previous efforts to create a comprehensive strategy for energy supply and usage across all relevant sectors. Developed using a Multi-Criteria Approach (MCA), the BNEP assesses policies from multiple perspectives, addressing financial, economic, environmental, technological, and social factors. Similarly, Jamaica's National Energy Policy 2009–2030, as noted by the Office of Utilities Regulation (OUR), seeks to optimize the country's energy resources through renewable energy development. It aims to enhance international competitiveness, energy security, and reduce carbon emissions, with a target of having 20% of the energy mix from renewable sources by 2030.

The government should implement Simplified Permitting Processes to expedite the approval process for renewable energy projects. This method would remove bureaucratic bottlenecks, accelerate project development, stimulate investment, and reduce overall installation expenses. Currently, obtaining permits in Jamaica can be cumbersome due to inefficient systems and a lack of transparency, which often leads to frustration. The application requirements and fees are frequently deterrents. The key challenge in simplifying this procedure is a lack of clear standards, which makes it difficult for applicants to grasp the requirements and criteria.

The Petroleum Corporation of Jamaica (PCJ) is the major organization in charge of implementing energy security and fuel diversification policies, as well as administering renewable energy permits. The Jamaica Public Service Company Limited (JPSCo) operates the National Electric Grid and, in collaboration with several Independent Power Producers (IPPs), manages the country's electrical power needs. The Rural Electrification Programme (REP) is in charge of bringing electricity to rural regions. It has erected 7000 kilometres of low-voltage distribution lines and electrified around 70,000 rural dwellings, supplying power to more than 90% of the island's population.

Another obstacle is the Jamaica Public Service corporation Ltd (JPS) exclusive licence, which grants the corporation unique rights to transport, distribute, and supply power across Jamaica for a 20-year period under the All-Island power Licence (2001). The government should consider investing in Grid Integration to improve the grid's ability to handle sources of clean energy. Upgrading the electricity grid to accommodate these sources will increase renewable energy consumption, manage intermittent power generation, offer energy storage, and enable bidirectional energy flow. Kolkowska (2023) emphasizes the importance of enhanced sensors, automation, and real-time data processing in integrating renewable energy.

These technologies enhance grid efficiency, reduce energy losses, and improve stability by monitoring and assessing grid conditions. Power grids are complex networks involving transmission lines, transformers, and distribution systems that deliver energy from power plants to end users, consisting of generation, transmission, and distribution components. The government should integrate key sectors to advance Jamaica's renewable energy goals.

This integration will foster a responsive legislative and regulatory environment that supports the growth of renewable energy. It will focus on creating, implementing, and refining a legislative framework to encourage renewable energy adoption. The integrated body should prioritize: (1) Research and development (R&D) in collaboration with public and private entities to advance renewable technologies, business models, and policies, and (2) Supporting the demonstration and commercialization of decentralized renewable technologies to enhance local energy use, security, and community benefits such as job creation and reduced transmission losses.

Another major barrier to Jamaica's efficiency targets is a lack of effective policy execution. The Ministry of Energy and Mining (2010) intends to solve this issue by implementing a continual monitoring and assessment programme. This initiative will engage partners from both the public and commercial sectors and will be consistent with Vision 2030 Jamaica's Monitoring and Evaluation Framework and the Whole of Government Business Strategy Process. The Ministry will utilize a variety of metrics to evaluate the performance of the National Renewable Energy Policy and lead any required policy changes. The Ministry of Energy and Mining (MEM) will lead the implementation of the Renewable Energy Policy in partnership with other government agencies, the corporate sector, universities, and non-governmental organizations.

The Petroleum Corporation of Jamaica (PCJ), a Ministry agency, and its Centre of Excellence for Renewable Energy (CERE) will support renewable energy initiatives. The Ministry of Energy and Mining (MEM) will prioritize establishing the requisite human resource competencies among implementing partners to improve understanding and access to renewable technology. Successful policy implementation will necessitate collaboration with other sectors such as agriculture, transportation, the environment, finance, and education. The Office of Utilities Regulation (OUR) will play a critical role in crafting laws for effective renewable energy deployment, as well as overseeing the regulatory framework for such efforts, safeguarding both consumers and investors.

The Scientific Research Council, in collaboration with the Office of the Prime Minister (Environmental Management Division), will oversee environmental management, land use, spatial planning, and waste management, particularly for waste-to-energy projects. They will collaborate with the National Environment and Planning Agency (NEPA) to provide environmental knowledge, ensure renewable energy production is ecologically sustainable, and examine the impact on greenhouse gas emissions. NEPA will also consider permit applications for renewable energy projects.

The National Environment and Planning Agency (NEPA) will ensure that renewable energy projects meet environmental requirements and laws. It will guarantee that these projects are designed and operated in a way that safeguards human health and the environment against hazardous emissions. NEPA will regularly assess the environmental performance of renewable energy installations and operations, including routine emissions assessments. The government will also ensure compliance and take legal action if infractions are found.

TECHNOLOGY AND INNOVATION

Promoting technology and innovation is crucial for advancing clean and efficient energy use. Technological advancements can make clean energy solutions more accessible and affordable, while also opening new possibilities for energy conservation. Key innovations include smart grids, which enhance electricity distribution efficiency, energy storage systems that store surplus renewable energy for later use, and energy-efficient appliances that consume less energy while delivering the same performance as their less efficient counterparts.

To meet the Net Zero Emissions (NZE) target by 2050, the rate of innovation in sustainable energy technologies must increase. While existing technologies can deliver the majority of the necessary CO_2 reductions by 2030, meeting the 2050 target will require new technologies that are not yet widely available but must emerge within this decade, particularly in difficult-to-decarbonize sectors such as heavy industry and long-distance transportation.

There is considerable opportunity for innovation to improve and lower the prices of renewable energy technology. This comprises both enhanced versions of traditional energy sources including solar, wind, biomass, hydro, and geothermal, as well as novel technologies and advancements in energy storage and integration. Many national and international policies prioritize renewable energy technology, and growing renewable energy is an essential component of most efforts for reducing greenhouse gas emissions and combating climate change.

Renewable energy solutions are becoming increasingly important as the world works to combat climate change and reduce reliance on polluting fossil fuels. These technologies are critical for sustainable development, which attempts to fulfil current demands while protecting future generations.

The idea of sustainable development, which originated in the 1980s, combines economic, social, and environmental considerations to assure a brighter future for everyone. It emphasizes on providing resources for a good quality of life while reducing environmental effect, ensuring that economic, social, and environmental factors are interrelated and mutually beneficial (Verma, 2023). Renewable energy technologies are critical to sustainable development because they reduce greenhouse gas emissions, improve energy security, and expand power availability to previously underserved areas. For example, renewable energy sources release 90 to 99% less greenhouse gases and 70 to 90% fewer pollutants than coal-fired power plants (Verma, 2023).

Investing in renewable energy technology promotes job creation and economic growth, both of which are critical for Jamaica's long-term advancement. Keyways in which renewable energy promotes sustainable development include:

1. Renewable energy sources, such as solar and wind power, reduce greenhouse gas emissions and ameliorate climate change by decreasing dependency on fossil fuels and lowering hazardous pollutants like CO_2.
2. Improving energy security: By utilizing locally available resources, renewable energy enhances energy security and reduces dependence on imported fuels, making energy supplies more reliable.
3. Providing access to energy: Renewable technologies can deliver energy to underserved communities, especially in developing countries, which helps alleviate poverty and improves living standards by enabling essential services like lighting and heating.
4. Job creation: The renewable energy sector, particularly in solar panel production and installation, creates numerous jobs and stimulates economic growth, contributing to the expansion of employment opportunities.

To meet Vision 2030s renewable energy targets, it is critical to fully use energy technologies. The two primary advantages of incorporating technology and innovation into renewable energy are (1) increased efficiency of renewable energy technologies and (2) larger social and economic acceptability of renewable energy systems (Wohlgemuth, 2023). Jamaica is ideally positioned for renewable energy growth due to its numerous resources, which include wind, biomass, mini-hydro, photovoltaic, and solar energy, as well as possibilities for waste-to-energy conversion, ocean thermal technology, and biofuels. Despite this, the absence of technology innovation is a key barrier to reaching Vision 2030. However, this does not exclude the government from implementing measures to solve this issue and promote Vision 2030.

The government should promote renewable energy research and development by devoting funding to advanced technologies such as enhanced photovoltaics, energy storage systems, and grid optimization. Local colleges and research institutes, such as the University of Technology and the University of the West Indies, should focus on these areas and include them in authorized courses to increase participation. Engaging young minds in STEM education at both the university and secondary levels is key because it encourages critical thinking, problem-solving, and creativity—all of which are necessary for promoting renewable energy and supporting national growth.

Notwithstanding this, a report entitled "The Renewable Energies Potential in Jamaica" (2005) identified several barriers to the expansion of renewable energy use in Jamaica, as follows: (1) Time-consuming administrative procedures related to RE project development (2) Lack of economically sound contractual arrangements (3) Imprecise legal formulations, Inadequate financial and fiscal incentives (e.g. duty and GCT exemptions or property tax rebates), and (4) Lack of dedicated grants or soft-loans for RE exploration.

The government should emphasize local production of renewable energy components including solar panels, wind turbines, and batteries. This strategy may minimize reliance on imports, generate jobs, and boost economic growth while building renewable energy infrastructure. Industrial not only creates well-paying employment, but it also promotes innovation in both the industrial and service industries. Improving infrastructure and technology for modern and sustainable energy may replace polluting fossil fuels with cleaner alternatives, diversify Jamaica's energy sources, improve energy security, and reduce the country's carbon footprint. Jamaica has already made progress in this area, having added the Old Harbor Power (190 MW) and Bogue Power Plant (201 MW) facilities (Planning Institute of Jamaica, 2022).

Flexibility and the capacity to respond swiftly to changing market conditions are critical for corporate success. Local manufacturing, or "in-house production," allows for quick adjustments and revisions in response to new ideas or product issues. This strategy reduces the need for long communications with faraway organizations, allowing for faster and more effective decision-making. For it to be effective in Jamaica's industrial sector, renewable electricity pricing should be based on averted costs, such as those associated with displaced power plants, rather than the cheapest option. Additionally, rates must be stable for a minimum of ten years, contain an incentive for social and environmental benefits, and be index-linked to both inflation and currency volatility. This method will appeal to operators and investors by delivering an acceptable return without increasing total power costs or being impacted by growing fossil fuel prices (Blair-Loy, 2005).

To reduce the costs of building industrial facilities, Jamaica could explore forging alliances with multinational businesses that share its objectives. For example, in 2017, the Bajan government welcomed Canadian company Deltro's solar panel manufacturing and solar farm project, with the goal of advancing renewable energy in the Caribbean and increasing the region's potential for residential and industrial solar energy development (New Energy Administration).

In addition to encouraging indigenous production, the Jamaican government should encourage energy storage technology. Investing in technologies such as batteries and pumped hydro storage is crucial to solving renewable energy's intermittent nature. These storage options will be critical to improving grid stability, dependability, and integration. Renewable energy, contrary to fossil fuels, produces clean electricity with no greenhouse gas emissions (National Grid, n.d.). By storing and using renewable energy, the country may minimize its reliance on higher-carbon-emitting sources such as coal, natural gas, and oil. Energy storage also prevents the wastage of excess renewable power, as it allows surplus energy to be stored rather than forcing a reduction in production to maintain system balance.

Encouraging Clean and Efficient Energy Consumption: Key Recommendations for Stakeholders

According to the data supplied, various variables must be addressed to ensure access to clean energy, particularly in low-income neighbourhoods. This entails increasing knowledge transmission through educational efforts that aim to provide citizens with information about clean and efficient energy use. It is critical that information is communicated clearly, particularly through public awareness campaigns and educational programmes. The fundamental goal is to better prepare people to make informed decisions. Furthermore, it is expected that these initiatives will reach households, schools, businesses, and communities, emphasizing the economic, health, and environmental benefits of using clean energy (International Energy Agency).

Another area that needs to be examined is the conversation that we need to have about how we better strengthen and regulate energy efficiency standards for encouraging clean and efficient energy consumption. It is therefore the hope that the Government of Jamaica will establish minimum energy performance standards for appliances, vehicles, and buildings, promoting the adoption of energy-efficient technologies that are shared with all communities. However, these standards can also better assist with the issue of market transformation by creating a level playing field, reducing energy waste, and stimulating innovation in the clean energy sector.

1. To enhance clean and efficient energy consumption, it is essential to prioritize access to financial support, particularly through government initiatives and the Jamaica Public Service (JPS). Such incentives may encompass tax credits, grants, subsidies, and low-interest loans aimed at facilitating energy-efficient upgrades and renewable energy installations. Additionally, there should be a concentrated effort on evaluating the costs associated with utilizing solar energy for electricity generation. By leveraging these incentives, individuals and businesses can mitigate initial expenses while improving their return on investment. This approach can also significantly motivate the adoption of cleaner and more efficient energy solutions.
2. A keyway to address the challenge of having access to electricity and finding better renewable energy is by ensuring that we spend a bit more time looking at the various policies that can be put in place with the assistance of the Jamaican government and non-governmental organizations (NGOs) have implemented policies to address electricity access, renewable energy deployment. The use of these policies will also help with providing financial incentives such as tariffs, minimum price for renewable energy sources with these interventions will make the process of having access to energy effective.
3. It is critical to look at policies that are better table towards construction that look at how buildings are planned, and with the use of these technologies, they are better able to look at subsidies for energy efficient appliances. Some of the policies include the National Energy Policy. This policy aims to provide a framework for Jamaica's sustainable energy development. It also aims to promote energy efficiency, diversify the energy mix, and increase the share of renewable energy sources.

4. While we also aim to drive these standards, it is also important that we also look at and promote smart technologies, such as smart grids, smart metres, and energy management systems, that can empower consumers to monitor and optimize their energy consumption. This is also critical at all households as we ensure that persons are better able to afford energy in real-time on energy usage and costs. Smart technologies enable individuals and businesses to make informed decisions that will also help citizens to be better able to adjust their behaviour accordingly.
5. In the long term, our objective is to enable households to invest more effectively in renewable energy while simultaneously promoting energy efficiency and encouraging behavioural changes. Achieving this goal necessitates enhanced collaboration among governments, businesses, non-governmental organizations, and various other stakeholders. Governments can play a crucial role by developing policies that encourage partnerships through platforms for dialogue and cooperation, facilitating the exchange of best practices, knowledge, and resources. Furthermore, improved collaboration is essential for formulating comprehensive energy policies, devising innovative solutions, and identifying the obstacles that low-income households must overcome to facilitate broader adoption of clean energy practices.

Conclusion

Energy efficiency is becoming increasingly important in Jamaica, which confronts problems in satisfying its energy requirements while lowering its carbon impact. With a population of roughly 3 million, Jamaica's reliance on imported fossil fuels has resulted in high energy prices, an unpredictable power supply, and environmental issues. However, the country has made tremendous progress towards renewable energy adoption through public awareness campaigns, business sector investments, and government measures. Jamaica is involved in a variety of regional renewable energy activities and should make use of international programmes such as the Renewable Energy & Energy Efficiency Partnership (REEP), which was founded by the British government in 2002, as well as Commonwealth initiatives. To enhance energy results, it is critical to address women's underrepresentation in technical energy sectors and decision-making positions.

Jamaica is making considerable gains in diversifying its energy sector as the government prepares to implement the island's ambitious Integrated

Resource Plan (IRP). The island is well on its way. Jamaica intends to produce 33% of its electricity from renewable sources by 2030, and the island already boasts strong renewable energy projects that serve as a firm foundation for the country's energy resource strategy. One example is WRB Energy Company's Clarendon-based 20-MW Content Solar Ltd. solar energy power producing facility. In Westmoreland, the largest photovoltaic (PV) power plant in Jamaica, the 51 MWp Paradise Park solar farm is one of the least expensive suppliers of electricity.

Also, the Wigton Windfarm at Rose Hill, Manchester, includes a 20.7 MW plant and an 18 MW expansion facility, making it one of the largest of its sort in the Caribbean (Loop News, 2021). Munro Wind Farm, operated by Jamaica Public Service (JPS), has the capacity to generate 3 MW of power, whereas Blue Mountain Renewable (BMR) Jamaica Wind generates 34 MW. The JPS Utility Company operates a 7.2-MW hydropower facility in Maggoty, St. Elizabeth.

Tackling gender stereotypes should begin in the classroom. Educational programmes must focus on reducing biases in teaching techniques and materials. Partnership with Technical Vocational Schools (TVET) and universities is also vital in encouraging girls to continue their education and training in energy-related sectors. On the other hand, energy sector organizations should evaluate the advantages of incorporating gender issues into their policy. Incorporating gender into human resource strategies, for example, can result in increased productivity, lower staff turnover and absenteeism, and greater retention of high-quality personnel. Promoting clean and efficient energy use is critical for achieving sustainable development and combatting climate change. Although numerous technologies and techniques can help achieve this aim, people and organizations continue to face a number of challenges to their adoption.

References

All-Island Electric Licence. (2001). *All-Island Electric Licence 2001*. Office of Utilities Regulation, Jamaica.

Asian Infrastructure Investment Bank. (2021). AIIB 2021 annual report and financials. https://www.aiib.org/en/news-events/annual-report/2021/home/index.htmlAIIB+2AIIB+2AIIB+2

Blair-Loy, M. (2005). *Competing devotions: Career and family among women executives*. Harvard University Press. https://doi.org/10.4159/9780674021594

CARICOM. (2020, October 15). *Standards and codes essential to the development of the CARICOM energy sector.* https://caricom.org/standards-codes-critical-to-caricom-energy-sector-development/

Castellanos-Sosa, F. A., Cabral, R., & Varella Mollick, A. (2022). Energy reform and energy consumption convergence in Mexico: A spatial approach. *Structural Change and Economic Dynamics, 61*, 336–350. https://doi.org/10.1016/j.strueco.2022.02.004 franciscocastellanos.com

Eddy, M. (2023, February 14). *European Union to ban gas-powered cars by 2035.* The New York Times. https://www.nytimes.com/2023/02/14/world/europe/eu-gas-powered-cars-ban.html

Frąckiewicz, M. (2023, March 21). *The importance of education and training in renewable energy.* TS2 SPACE. https://ts2.space/en/the-importance-of-education-and-training-in-renewable-energy/

George, V. (2024, August 8). *China to set 70 new standards for emissions reductions and carbon capture.* Carbon Herald. https://carbonherald.com/china-to-set-70-new-standards-for-emissions-reductions-and-carbon-capture/#:~:text=The%20country%E2%80%99s%20top%20economic%20planning%20agency%20announced%20plans,China%20to%20measure%20and%20reduce%20their%20carbon%20emissions

Hughes, M. (2018, December 10). *Why access to energy should be a basic human right.* Forbes. https://www.forbes.com/sites/mikehughes1/2018/12/10/why-access-to-energy-should-be-a-basic-human-right/

IRENA. (2022). *Fostering livelihoods with decentralised renewable energy.* https://www.irena.org/-/media/Files/IRENA/Agency/Publication/2022/Jan/IRENA_Livelihood_Decentralised_Renewables_2022.pdf

Jamaica Information Service. (2015). *Jamaica Information Service—The voice of Jamaica.* https://jis.gov.jm/ YouTube+2Jamaica Information Service+2 Jamaica Information Service+2

Joseph, J. (2023, July 10). *The growing importance of energy efficiency in Jamaica.* CARILEC. https://www.carilec.org/the-growing-importance-of-energy-efficiency-in-jamaica/

Kumar, M. (2020, January 21). *Social, economic, and environmental impacts of renewable energy resources.* IntechOpen. https://www.intechopen.com/chapters/70874

Loop News. (2021, July 2). *Gender equality must be at the heart of recovery efforts, experts say. Loop News.* https://www.loopnews.com/content/gender-equality-must-be-at-the-heart-of-recovery-efforts-experts-say/

Loy, D., & Coviello, M. F. (2005, June). *Renewable energies potential in Jamaica* (Project document). United Nations Economic Commission for Latin America and the Caribbean (ECLAC), in collaboration with the Ministry of Commerce, Science and Technology of Jamaica.

Marsh, M. (2023). *The Global Risks Report 2023.* https://www.marsh.com/en/risks/global-risk/insights/global-risks-report-2023.html Marsh+1Marsh+1

Marshall, S., & Koon Koon, R. (2021). Barbados towards 100% renewable energy: Case scenarios for 2030 national energy target plans. *The West Indian Journal of Engineering, 44*(1), 11–17.

McIntosh, D. (2015, January 19). *Strong take-up of Renewable Energy Policy*. Jamaica Information Service. https://jis.gov.jm/strong-take-renewable-energy-policy/

Ministry of Energy and Mining, Jamaica. (2010). *National renewable energy policy 2009–2030: Creating a sustainable future*. https://www.mset.gov.jm/wpcontent/uploads/2019/07/Draft-Renewable-Energy-Policy_0.pdf   mset.gov.jm+1mset.gov.jm+1

Moe to spend $60 million on solar energy in schools. (2020, February 13). News I Jamaica Gleaner. https://jamaica-gleaner.com/article/news/20200213/moe-spend-60-million-solar-energy-schools

Morris, A. (2020, February 13). *$60 million to privide solar energy in schools*. Jamaica Information Service. https://jis.gov.jm/60-million-to-privide-solar-energy-in-schools/

National Grid Group. (n.d.). *What is renewable energy storage (and why is it important for reaching net zero)?* https://www.nationalgrid.com/stories/energy-explained/what-is-renewable-energy-storage#:~:text=A%20key%20benefit%20of%20being,that's%20needed%20at%20the%20time

Office of the Prime Minister, Jamaica. (2023). *Daryl Vaz MP—Minister of Science, Energy, Telecommunications and Transport*. https://opm.gov.jm/cabinet_ministers/daryl-vaz/mset.gov.jm+2opm.gov.jm+2maritimejamaica.com+2

Planning Institute of Jamaica. (2022). *Message from the Director-General*. https://www.vision2030.gov.jm/blog/message-from-the-director-general-planning-institute-of-jamaicapioj/vision2030.gov.jm

Pietrapertosa, F., Tancredi, M., Giordano, M., Cosmi, C., & Salvia, M. (2021). How to prioritize energy efficiency interventions in municipal public buildings to decrease CO_2 emissions? A case study from Italy. *International Journal of Environmental Research and Public Health, 18*(7), 3760. https://doi.org/10.3390/ijerph18073760 PubMed

Philipp, J. (2023, May 18). *The state of renewable energy in Jamaica*. The Borgen Project. https://borgenproject.org/renewable-energy-in-jamaica/

Richards, D., & Yabar, H. (2022). Potential of renewable energy in Jamaica's power sector: Feasibility analysis of biogas production for electricity generation. *Sustainability, 14*(11), 6457. https://doi.org/10.3390/su141164571DEAS/RePEc

Robertson, K. (2023, January 10). *Mia Mottley: Caribbean, or World leader?* Americas Quarterly. https://www.americasquarterly.org/article/mia-mottley-caribbean-or-world-leader/#:~:text=Mottley%2C%2057%2C%20has%20become%20a,attention%20to%20her%20outspoken%20style

U.S. Energy Information Administration - EIA - *independent statistics and analysis*. (2022, December 27). Wind energy and the environment - U.S. Energy Information Administration (EIA). https://www.eia.gov/energyexplained/wind/wind-energy-and-the-environment.php

Verma, A. (2023). Promoting energy and resource recovery from livestock waste. *Journal of Environmental Management, 325*, 116389. https://doi.org/10.1016/j.jenvman.2022.116389 ScienceDirect+1ScienceDirect+1

William, R. (2021, March 15). *Leveraging energy from renewable sources key to creating new Jamaica*. Jamaica Information Services. https://jis.gov.jm/leveraging-energy-from-renewable-sources-key-to-creating-new-jamaica-minister-vaz/

World Economic Forum. (2022). *Annual report 2021–2022*. https://www.weforum.org/publications/annual-report-2021-2022/ World Economic Forum+1World Economic Forum+1

World Health Organization. (2019). *World health statistics 2019: Monitoring health for the SDGs*. https://www.who.int/publications/i/item/9789241565707 World Health Organization (WHO)

Wohlgemuth, N. (2023). Decentralized power generation: Community microgrids with ocean energy. *Renewable and Sustainable Energy Reviews, 159*, 112203. https://doi.org/10.1016/j.rser.2022.112203

Yabar, H., Nhiakao, K., & Mizunoya, T. (2022). Cost-benefit analysis of the Nam Che 1 hydropower plant, Thathom District, Laos: An ex-post analysis. *Sustainability, 14*(6), 3178. https://doi.org/10.3390/su14063178

REFERENCES

Abdourahman, O. I. (2010). Time poverty: A contributor to women's poverty? *The African Statistical Journal, 11*, 1–22.
Adisa, P. O. (2020, December 11). *Let us end gender-based violence*. The Gleaner. https://jamaica-gleaner.com/article/commentary/20201211/opal-palmer-adisa-let-usend-gender-based-violence
All-Island Electric Licence. (2001). *All-Island Electric Licence 2001*. Office of Utilities Regulation, Jamaica.
Anderson, W., White, V., & Finney, A. D. (2012). Coping with low incomes and cold homes. *Energy Policy, 49*, 40–52. https://doi.org/10.1016/j.enpol.2012.01.002
Asian Infrastructure Investment Bank. (2021). AIIB 2021 annual report and financials. https://www.aiib.org/en/news-events/annual-report/2021/home/index.htmlAIIB+2AIIB+2AIIB+2
Askwbcaribbean: Talking energy, finding solutions. (2022, October 22). World Bank. https://www.worldbank.org/en/events/2022/10/11/caribbean-talking-energy-finding-solutions#:~:text=of%20Biomass%2FWTE.-,With%20the%20global%20oil%20prices%20on%20the%20rise%2C%20the%20already,easing%20in%202023%20and%202024
Barnes, D. F. (1995). Consequences of energy policies for the urban poor. *Energy Policy, 23*(9), 739–750.
Barrett, J. (2019, October 10). 50m reasons why - Reid, Pinnock, three others charged in ministry, CMU fraud. *The Gleaner*. https://jamaica-gleaner.com/article/lead-stories/20191010/50m-reasons-why-reid-pinnock-three-others-charged-ministry-cmu-fraud#google_vignette

Beckford, M. (2018). *Study underway to select local crops for biofuel production.* Jamaica Observer. https://advancedbiofuelsusa.info/tag/jamaica

Bennett Marsh, E. (2022, March 6). *OUR provides regulatory balance.* The Gleaner. https://jamaica-gleaner.com/article/commentary/20220306/elizabeth-bennett-marsh-ourprovides-regulatory-balance

BENNETT Senior business reporter bennettk@jamaicaobserver.com, K. (2024, March 27). *Dismantle JPS monopoly.* Jamaica Observer. https://www.jamaicaobserver.com/2024/03/27/dismantle-jps-monopoly/

Berik, G. (2017). *Toward more inclusive measures of economic well-being.* International Labour Organization. https://www.ilo.org/sites/default/files/wcmsp5/groups/public/@dgreports/@cabinet/documents/publication/wcms_649127.pdf

Beuermann, D. W., et al. (2023). *Title of the work.* Publisher.

Beuermann, D. W., et al. (2024). *Title of the work.* Publisher.

Bishop, H. (2022). *Custos Rotulorum of saint James, Jamaica.* https://www.custosofstjamesja.com/

Blair-Loy, M. (2005). *Competing devotions: Career and family among women executives.* Harvard University Press. https://doi.org/10.4159/9780674021594

Bove, T. (2021). *Ecofeminism: Where gender and climate change intersect.* Earth.Org. https://earth.org/ecofeminism/

Brenner, J. (1989). Gender and social reproduction: Historical perspectives. *Annual Review of Sociology, 15,* 381–404. JSTOR.

Brown, K., et al. (2020). *Toward a gender diverse workforce in the renewable energy transition.* https://www.researchgate.net/publication/306314469_Toward_a_gender_diverse_workforce_in_the_renewable_energy_transition

Bruno, D., Ferrara, M., D'Alessandro, F., & Mandelli, A. (2022). The Italian Company Cassina as a case study on the role of design in the furniture industry's CE transition. https://www.mdpi.com/2071-1050/14/15/9168

Bryan, G. A. (2023, February 8). Women-led entrepreneurship in Jamaica: The dynamics between education and work. *UN Women Caribbean.* https://caribbean.unwomen.org/en/stories/press-release/2022/12/afro-descendant-women-entrepreneurs-benefit-from-business-development-bootcamp-in-jamaica

Buckingham, S. (2015). *Gender and the environment.* Routledge. https://www.routledge.com/Gender-and-the-Environment/Buckingham/p/book/9780415530446

Campbell, A. (2016). Price and income elasticities of electricity demand: Evidence from Jamaica. *Energy Economics, 56,* 1–10.

Cao, C., Duan, H., & Ng, L. L. (2023). The impact of gender inequality in higher education on female employment. *Journal of Education, Humanities and Social Sciences (EPHHR), 8,* 2355.

Caribbean Policy Research Institute (CAPRI). (2021). *The real cost of unpaid care and domestic work.* https://www.capricaribbean.org/sites/default/files/documents/whocarestherealcostofunpaidcareanddomesticwork.pdf

CAPRI. (2023, February 1). *Fair pay: The wage gap barrier to women's empowerment.* Caribbean Policy Research Institute (CAPRI). https://capricaribbean.org/document/fair-pay-wage-gap-barrier-womens-empowerment#:~:text=Women%20are%20still%20generally%20poorer,is%20the%20gender%20wage%20gap

Caribbean Development Bank. (2018). *Integrating gender equality into the energy sector.* https://www.caribank.org/sites/default/files/publicationresources/CDB8_INTEGRATING%20GENDER%20EQUALITY%20INTO%20THE%20ENERGY%20SECTOR_final.pdf

CARICOM. (2020, October 15). *Standards and codes essential to the development of the CARICOM energy sector.* https://caricom.org/standards-codes-critical-to-caricom-energy-sector-development/

Castellanos-Sosa, F. A., Cabral, R., & Varella Mollick, A. (2022). Energy reform and energy consumption convergence in Mexico: A spatial approach. *Structural Change and Economic Dynamics, 61*, 336–350. https://doi.org/10.1016/j.strueco.2022.02.004 franciscocastellanos.com

Chant, S. (2003). *The 'engendering' of poverty analysis in developing regions: Progress since the United Nations Decade for Women, and priorities for the future* (New Working Paper Series No. 11). Gender Institute, London School of Economics and Political Science. http://eprints.lse.ac.uk/573/

Children's Bureau. (2023). *A father's impact on child development.* https://calendar-dffcdads.org/fathers-impact-on-child-development/calendar-dffcdads.org

Clark. (2012). *Ecofeminism - an overview.* ScienceDirect Topics. https://www.sciencedirect.com/topics/social-sciences/ecofeminism#:~:text=Ecofeminists%20view%20patriarchy%20as%20responsible,to%20be%20used%20and%20discarded

Clemente, J. (2015, January 22). End energy poverty and empower women. *Forbes.* https://www.forbes.com/sites/judeclemente/2015/01/22/alleviating-energy-poverty-and-empowering-females/

Coaston, J. (2019, May 20). *The intersectionality wars.* Vox. https://www.vox.com/the-highlight/2019/5/20/18542843/intersectionality-conservatism-law-race-gender-discrimination

Conference on Trade and Development of the United Nation. (2019). *The role of science, technology and innovation in promoting renewable energy by 2030.* https://unctad.org/system/files/official-document/dtlstict2019d2_en.pdf

Davis, A. (2024, July 17). *Time to rethink our energy infrastructure.* Jamaica Observer. https://www.jamaicaobserver.com/2024/07/17/time-rethink-energy-infrastructure/

Denton, F. (2001). Gendered impacts of climate change: A human security issue. *Energy Policy, 39*(6), 1037–1046.

Denton, F. (2002). Climate change vulnerability, impacts, and adaptation: Why does gender matter? *Gender & Development, 10*(2), 10–20.

Douglas, B., & Hussain, S. (2018). *Measuring the Benefits of Energy Access: A Handbook for Development Practitioners.* https://doi.org/10.18235/0001459.

Duflo, E. (2012). Women empowerment and economic development. *Journal of Economic Literature, 50*(4), 1051–1079. https://doi.org/10.1257/jel.50.4.1051

Duncan-Price, I., Merusi, S., & Haarr, R. (2021). *Gender-responsive socioeconomic study on the impact of COVID-19 on women in business and women entrepreneurs in Jamaica.* UN Women Caribbean. https://caribbean.unwomen.org/en/materials/publications/2021/7/gender-responsive-socioeconomic-study-on-the-impact-of-covid-19-onbusinesswomen-in-jamaica_caribbean

Dutta, S., Kooijman, A., & Cecelski, E. (2017). *Energy access and gender: Getting the right balance.* ENERGIA, International Network on Gender and Sustainable Energy. https://www.energia.org/cm2/wp-content/uploads/2016/06/ENERGIA-news-16.pdf

Eckholm, E. (1975). *The other energy crisis: Firewood.* Worldwatch Paper 1.

Eddy, M. (2023, February 14). *European Union to ban gas-powered cars by 2035.* The New York Times. https://www.nytimes.com/2023/02/14/world/europe/eu-gas-powered-cars-ban.html

Elias, R. J., & Victor, D. G. (2005). *Energy transitions in developing countries: A review of concepts and literature* (Working Paper No. 40). Program on Energy and Sustainable Development, Stanford University.

Energy Sector Management Assistance Programme (ESMAP). (1999). *Energy services for the world's poor.* World Bank.

ENERGIA. (2017). *The Gender and Energy Research Programme: Policy Brief #1.* https://www.energia.org/assets/2017/03/Policybrief-Energia-March-GERP-2017-final-lr.pdf

ENERGIA Group. (2020). *Energia Group's top news stories of 2020.* https://www.energiagroup.com/newsmedia/energia-groups-top-new-stories-of-2020/

ENERGIA. (n.d.). *Women's economic empowerment program.* Retrieved December 1, 2024, from https://energia.org/impact-area/womens-economic-empowerment/

Energy Democracy Climate Justice Alliance. (2023, July 10). *Climate Justice Alliance.* https://climatejusticealliance.org/workgroup/energy-democracy/#:~:text=What%20is%20Energy%20Democracy%3F,well%2Dbeing%20for%20all%20peoples

Energy poverty. (n.d.). Habitat for Humanity https://www.habitat.org/emea/about/what-we-do/residential-energy-efficiency-households/energy-poverty

Energy poverty. (n.d.). Energy poverty - an overview | ScienceDirect Topics. https://www.sciencedirect.com/topics/social-sciences/energy-poverty#:~:text=According%20to%20the%20IEA%20%5B45,biomass%20for%20cooking%20and%20heating

Ensari, M. Ş. (2017). A study on the differences of entrepreneurship potential among generations. *Research Journal of Business and Management, 4*, 52–62. https://doi.org/10.17261/Pressacademia.2017.370

Environmental impact of renewable energy-A value chain approach - AIIB blog. (2021, November 17). AIIB. https://www.aiib.org/en/news-events/media-center/blog/2021/Environmental-Impact-of-Renewable-Energy-A-Value-Chain-Approach.html

European Parliament. (2021, June). Gender equality: Economic value of care from the perspective. https://www.europarl.europa.eu/RegData/etudes/STUD/2021/694784/IPOL_STU(2021)694784_EN.pdf

Evans, H. L. (1999). Gender and Achievement in Secondary Education in Jamaica: Kingston Policy Development Unit.

Feenstra, G. (2020). Gender and energy justice: A framework for policy development in the Caribbean. *Journal of Energy & Development, 46*(2), 145–163.

Finnamore, E. (2023, January 21). *Social Reproduction Theory and women in society.* Rupture. https://rupture.ie/articles/social-reproduction-theory-and-women-in-society

Fox, A. (2023, May 16). U.S. State Department issues warning against traveling to these popular Caribbean and South American countries. *Travel + Leisure.*

Frąckiewicz, M. (2023, March 21). *The importance of education and training in renewable energy.* TS2 SPACE. https://ts2.space/en/the-importance-of-education-and-training-in-renewable-energy/

Fraser, H. (n.d.). Perspectives in health: Health and wealth in Paradise. https://www3.paho.org/english/dd/pin/Number20_article06.htm

Gender Development, theories of - Miller - Wiley Online Library. (n.d.). https://onlinelibrary.wiley.com/doi/10.1002/9781118663219.wbegss590

George, V. (2024, August 8). *China to set 70 new standards for emissions reductions and carbon capture.* Carbon Herald. https://carbonherald.com/china-to-set-70-new-standards-for-emissions-reductions-and-carbon-capture/#:~:text=The%20country%E2%80%99s%20top%20economic%20planning%20agency%20announced%20plans,China%20to%20measure%20and%20reduce%20their%20carbon%20emissions

Gibson, V., & Dyer, J. (2018). Project Juno: Advancing gender equality in physics careers in higher education in the United Kingdom. *Proceedings of Science, 314*, 555. https://doi.org/10.22323/1.314.0555

Goal 5 achieve gender equality and empower all women and girls. (n.d.). https://www.pioj.gov.jm/wp-content/uploads/2022/10/VNR_Goal_5.pdf

González-Eguino, M. (2015). Energy poverty: An overview. *Renewable and Sustainable Energy Reviews, 47*, 377–385.

Gordon-Strachan, G., et al. (2014). Female gender is a social determinant of diabetes in the Caribbean. *International Journal of Environmental Research and Public Health, 11*(9), 9403–9412.

Gould, E., Schieder, J., & Geier, K. (2016, October 20). What is the gender pay gap and is it real? The complete guide to how women are paid less than men and why it can't be explained away. Economic Policy Institute. https://www.epi.org/publication/what-is-the-gender-pay-gap-and-is-it-real/

Guevara, Z., Mendoza-Tinoco, D., & Silva, C. (2023). The theoretical peculiarities of energy poverty research: A systematic literature review. *Energy Research & Social Science, 105*, 103274. https://doi.org/10.1016/j.erss.2023.103274

Gunningham, N. (2013). Managing the energy trilemma: The case of Indonesia. *Energy Policy, 54*, 184–193.

Guruswamy, L. (2011). Energy poverty. *Annual Review of Environment and Resources, 36*(1), 139–161. https://doi.org/10.1146/annurev-environ-040610-090118

Harcourt, W., & Nelson, I. L. (Eds.). (2015). *Practising feminist political ecologies: Moving beyond the "Green Economy"*. Zed Books. UN Women.

Headly, J. (2021). *Title of the work*. Publisher.

Helper, S., Krueger, T., & Howard, W. (2021, February). Why does manufacturing matter? Which manufacturing matters? https://www.brookings.edu/wp-content/uploads/2016/06/0222_manufacturing_helper_krueger_wial.pdf

Hendrick, L., Opdenakker, M. C., & Van der Vaart, W. (2023). Students' academic engagement during COVID-19 times: A mixed-methods study into relatedness and loneliness during the pandemic. *Frontiers in Psychology, 14*, 1221003. https://doi.org/10.3389/fpsyg.2023.1221003. PMID: 37744611; PMCID: PMC10514504.

Ho, E. W., Strohmeier-Breuning, S., Rossanese, M., Charron, D., Pennise, D., & Graham, J. P. (2021). Diverse health, gender and economic impacts from domestic transport of water and solid fuel: A systematic review. *International Journal of Environmental Research and Public Health, 18*(19), 10355. https://doi.org/10.3390/ijerph181910355. PMID: 34639655; PMCID: PMC8507830.

Hodges, P.-G. (2016, June 17). *Jamaica Information Service – the voice of Jamaica*. Health Ministry Supports Fight Against Unhealthy Eating. https://jis.gov.jm/

Hedges, S. B., Cohen, W. B., Timyan, J., & Yang, Z. (2018). Haiti's biodiversity threatened by nearly complete loss of primary forest. *Proceedings of the National Academy of Sciences of the United States of America, 115*(46), 11850–11855. https://doi.org/10.1073/pnas.1809753115

Hirsh, R., & Koomey, J. (2015). Electricity Consumption and Economic Growth: A New Relationship with Significant Consequences?. *The Electricity Journal. 28*. https://doi.org/10.1016/j.tej.2015.10.002.

REFERENCES

Hoominfar, E. (2021). Gender socialization. In W. Leal Filho, A. M. Azul, L. Brandli, P. G. Özuyar, & T. Wall (Eds.), *Gender equality: Encyclopedia of the UN Sustainable Development Goals* (pp. 1–10). Springer. https://doi.org/10.1007/978-3-319-95687-9_13

Hughes, M. (2018, December 10). *Why access to energy should be a basic human right*. Forbes. https://www.forbes.com/sites/mikehughes1/2018/12/10/why-access-to-energy-should-be-a-basic-human-right/

Huyer, S., & Westholm, G. (2001). *Gender and climate change: A training manual*. International Union for Conservation of Nature (IUCN).

IDB Invest. (2022). Sustainability report 2022. *Inter-American Investment Corporation*. https://idbinvest.org/en/sustainability/sustainability_report_2022

Iea. (n.d.). *Energy and gender – topics*. IEA. https://www.iea.org/topics/energy-and-gender

Indrawati, S. M. (2023). *6 Human capital development and gender equality in Indonesia*. Gender Equality and Diversity in Indonesia: Identifying Progress and Challenges, 93.

International Energy Agency (IEA). (2017). World Energy Outlook 2017. https://www.iea.org/reports/world-energy-outlook-2017

International Energy Agency (IEA). (2021). *Energy and gender*. https://www.iea.org/topics/energy-and-gender

International Energy Agency. (2022). https://www.iea.org/reports/renewables-2022

International Energy Agency. (n.d.). *Innovation - Energy System*. https://www.iea.org/energy-system/decarbonisation-enablers/innovation

International Labour Organization. (2018). Greening with jobs: World Employment Social Outlook 2018. ILO.

International Labour Organization (ILO). (2019). *ILOSTAT: Statistics on women*. https://ilostat.ilo.org/

International Labour Organization (2019). *Promoting employment opportunities for people with disabilities*. https://www.ilo.org/wcmsp5/groups/public/%2D%2D-ed_emp/%2D%2D-ifp_skills/documents/publication/wcms_735531.pdf

Institute of Medicine and National Research Council. (2015). *Transforming the workforce for children birth through age 8: A unifying foundation*. The National Academies Press.

International Renewable Energy Agency. (2019). Renewable energy: A gender perspective. IRENA.

IRENA. (2022). Fostering livelihoods with decentralised renewable energy. https://www.irena.org/-/media/Files/IRENA/Agency/Publication/2022/Jan/IRENA_Livelihood_Decentralised_Renewables_2022.pdf

International Monetary Fund. (2020). *Jamaica and the IMF*. https://www.imf.org/en/Countries/JAM

Jagoe, K., Rossanese, M., Charron, D., Rouse, J., Waweru, F., Waruguru, M., Delapena, S., Piedrahita, R., Livingston, K., & Ipe, J. (2020). Sharing the burden: Shifts in family time use, agency and gender dynamics after introduction of new cookstoves in rural Kenya. *Energy Research & Social Science, 64*, 101413. https://doi.org/10.1016/j.erss.2019.101413

Jamaica Information Service. (2015). Jamaica Information Service—The voice of Jamaica. https://jis.gov.jm/ YouTube+2Jamaica Information Service+2 Jamaica Information Service+2

Jamaica Information Service (JIS). (2018). *Energy news.* https://jis.gov.jm/news/?category=energy

Jamaica Information Service. (2019). *Energy news.* https://jis.gov.jm/news/?category=energy

Jamaica Information Service. (2022). *Government to pay 20 per cent of electricity bill for low-income households.* https://jis.gov.jm/government-to-pay-20-per-cent-of-electricity-bill-for-low-income-households/

Jayaweera, S. A. A., et al. (1989). The effect of particle size on the combustion of Weardale coal. *Fuel, 68*(12), 1561–1565.

Jessel, S., Sawyer, S., & Hernández, D. (2019). Energy, poverty, and health in climate change: A comprehensive review of an emerging literature. *Frontiers in Public Health, 7*, 357. https://doi.org/10.3389/fpubh.2019.00357

Jimenez, M. P., DeVille, N. V., Elliott, E. G., Schiff, J. E., Wilt, G. E., Hart, J. E., & James, P. (2021). Associations between nature exposure and health: A review of the evidence. *International Journal of Environmental Research and Public Health, 18*(9), 4790. https://doi.org/10.3390/ijerph18094790

Joseph, J. (2023, July 10). *The growing importance of energy efficiency in Jamaica.* CARILEC. https://www.carilec.org/the-growing-importance-of-energy-efficiency-in-jamaica/

Kaygusuz, K. (2011). Energy services and energy poverty for sustainable rural development. *Renewable and Sustainable Energy Reviews, 15*(2), 936–947.

Kelsey Thomas Observer Online reporter thomask@jamaicaobserver.com , writer , H. G. B. O., & KASEY WILLIAMS Observer staff reporter kaseyw@jamaicaobserver.com . (2022, March 11). *JSIF $50-M grant to support Community Enterprises.* Jamaica Observer. https://www.jamaicaobserver.com/2022/03/10/jsif-50-m-grant-to-support-community-enterprises/#google_vignette

Knoth, G. (2015, July 9). *A classroom's worst nightmare? Energy poverty.* ONE.org US. https://www.one.org/us/stories/a-classrooms-worst-nightmare-energy-poverty/

Kumar, M. (2020, January 21). *Social, economic, and environmental impacts of renewable energy resources.* IntechOpen. https://www.intechopen.com/chapters/70874

Laxmi, V., Parikh, J., Karmakar, S., & Dabrase, P. (2003). *Household energy, women's hardship and health impacts in rural Rajasthan, India: Need for sustainable energy solutions* (pp. 50–68). Energy for Sustainable Development. https://www.sciencedirect.com/science/article/pii/S0973082608600370

Lindwall, C. (2022). *What are the effects of climate change?*. Effects of Climate Change-ImpactsandExamples.https://www.nrdc.org/stories/what-are-effects-climate-change

Loop News. (2021, July 2). Gender equality must be at the heart of recovery efforts, experts say. *Loop News.* https://www.loopnews.com/content/gender-equality-must-be-at-the-heart-of-recovery-efforts-experts-say/

Loy, D., & Coviello, M. F. (2005, June). *Renewable energies potential in Jamaica* (Project document). United Nations Economic Commission for Latin America and the Caribbean (ECLAC), in collaboration with the Ministry of Commerce, Science and Technology of Jamaica.

Maertens, L., & Stork, A. (2017, October 9). *The real story of Haiti's forests.* Books & ideas. https://booksandideas.net/The-Real-Story-of-Haiti-s-Forests

Makan, A. (1995). Power for women and men: Towards a gendered approach to domestic energy policy and planning in South Africa. *Third World Planning Review, 17*(2), 183–198. https://doi.org/10.3828/twpr.17.2.y951502074p2w545

Marsh, J. (2023, May 22). *The state of renewable energy in Jamaica.* The Borgen Project. https://borgenproject.org/renewable-energy-in-jamaica/

Marsh, M. (2023). *The Global Risks Report 2023.* https://www.marsh.com/en/risks/global-risk/insights/global-risks-report-2023.html Marsh+1Marsh+1

Marshall, S., & Koon Koon, R. (2021). Barbados towards 100% renewable energy: Case scenarios for 2030 national energy target plans. *The West Indian Journal of Engineering, 44*(1), 11–17.

Martins, A., Madaleno, M., & Dias, M. F. (2021). Women vs men: Who performs better on energy literacy? *International Journal of Sustainable Energy Planning and Management, 32*, 37–46. https://doi.org/10.5278/ijsepm.6516

McIntosh, D. (2015, January 19). *Strong take-up of Renewable Energy Policy.* Jamaica Information Service. https://jis.gov.jm/strong-take-renewable-energy-policy/

McIntosh, D. (2018, November 26). *Home.* Vision 2030. https://www.vision2030.gov.jm/

McKenzie, V. (2023, November 27). *Jamaica to go nuclear in bid to lower costs, end energy poverty - our Today.* Our Today -. https://our.today/jamaica-to-go-nuclear-in-bid-to-lower-costs-end-energy-poverty/

Middlemiss, L. (2022, July 1). Who is vulnerable to energy poverty in the Global North.... https://wires.onlinelibrary.wiley.com/doi/full/10.1002/wene.455

Miller, C. (2016). *A review of gender, social equity and low-carbon energy.* https://www.sciencedirect.com/science/article/pii/S2214629620303492

Ministry of Energy and Mining, Jamaica. (2010). *National renewable energy policy 2009–2030: Creating a sustainable future.* https://www.mset.gov.jm/wpcontent/uploads/2019/07/Draft-Renewable-Energy-Policy_0.pdf mset.gov.jm+1mset.gov.jm+1

Ministry of Energy Mozambique, & Partners. (2012). *Mozambique's ambitious energy strategy at 'golden moment' in the fight against poverty.* https://www.worldbank.org/en/news/feature/2012/04/04/mozambiques-ambitious-energy-strategy-at-golden-moment-in-the-fight-against-poverty

Ministry of Health & Wellness. (2018). *Vitals – A quarterly report of the Ministry of Health (May 2018).* https://www.moh.gov.jm/data/vitals-a-quarterly-report-of-the-ministry-of-health-may-2018/

Ministry of Science, Energy and Technology (MSET). (2019). *Jamaica Energy Balance 2019.* https://www.mset.gov.jm/wp-content/uploads/2019/06/Jamaica-Energy-Balance-2019.pdf

Modi, V., McDade, S., Lallement, D., & Saghir, J. (2005). *Energy services for the Millennium Development Goals.* United Nations Development Programme, UN Millennium Project, samy and World Bank.

Moe to spend $60 million on solar energy in schools. (2020, February 13). News | Jamaica Gleaner. https://jamaica-gleaner.com/article/news/20200213/moe-spend-60-million-solar-energy-schools

Mohammed, G. F., & Hashish, R. K. H. (2015). Sexual violence against females and its impact on their sexual function. Egyptian *Journal of Forensic Sciences,* 5(3), 96–102. https://doi.org/10.1016/j.ejfs.2014.08.004

Mokate, K. M. (Ed.). (2004). *Women's participation in social development: Experiences from Asia, Latin America, and the Caribbean.* Inter-American Development Bank. https://doi.org/10.18235/0012299

Momodu, S. (2023, March 5). *The Anglo-Ashanti wars (1823–1900).* https://www.blackpast.org/global-african-history/anglo-ashanti-wars-1823-1900/

Morris, A. (2020, February 13). *$60 million to privide solar energy in schools.* Jamaica Information Service. https://jis.gov.jm/60-million-to-privide-solar-energy-in-schools/

Munien, S., & Ahmed, F. (2012). A gendered perspective on energy poverty and livelihoods–Advancing the Millennium Development Goals in developing countries. *Agenda, 26*(1), 112–123. https://doi.org/10.1080/10130950.2012.665146

Munsell, M. (2017, April 4). *4 facts you should know about the Caribbean Solar Market.* Greentech Media. https://www.greentechmedia.com/articles/read/four-facts-you-should-know-about-the-caribbean-solar-market

Murphy, J. (2022, April 26). *Pollution danger.* Lead Stories | Jamaica Gleaner. https://jamaica-gleaner.com/article/lead-stories/20220426/pollution-danger

National Conference of State Legislatures. (n.d.). *Report energy justice and the energy transition.* https://www.ncsl.org/energy/energy-justice-and-the-energy-transition#:~:text=Building%20off%20the%20tenets%20of,nationality%2C%20income%20or%20geographic%20location

National Grid Group. (n.d.). *What is renewable energy storage (and why is it important for reaching net zero)?* https://www.nationalgrid.com/stories/energy-explained/what-is-renewable-energy-storage#:~:text=A%20key%20benefit%20of%20being,that's%20needed%20at%20the%20time

National Renewable Energy Laboratory. (2019). [*Title of the report*]. [URL]

Newenergyadmin. (2017, March 24). *Barbados to get solar panel manufacturing plant and solar farm.* New Energy Events. https://newenergyevents.com/barbados-to-get-solar-power-manufacturing-plant-and-solarfarm/#:~:text=General%20Secretary%20of%20the%20ruling,solar%20farm%20in%20this%20country

Nyandoro, M. (2024). Water in Botswana: Selective distribution of a finite commodity among indigenes (San), African villages and non-indigenous white minority communities, 1880s–2020. *The Dyke, 17*(2), Article 8. https://doi.org/10.10520/ejc-dyke_v17_n2_a8

Office of the Prime Minister. (2018, October 17). *Jamaica to increase renewables target to 50% – PM Holness.* JIS Jamaica. https://jis.gov.jm/jamaica-to-increase-renewables-targets-to-50-pm-holness/

Office of the Prime Minister, Jamaica. (2023). *Daryl Vaz MP—Minister of Science, Energy, Telecommunications and Transport.* https://opm.gov.jm/cabinet_ministers/daryl-vaz/mset.gov.jm+2opm.gov.jm+2maritimejamaica.com+2

Oliveras, L., Peralta, A., Palència, L., Gotsens, M., López, M. J., Artazcoz, L., Borrell, C., & Marí-Dell'Olmo, M. (2020). Energy poverty and health: Trends in the European Union before and during the economic crisis, 2007–2016. *Health & Place, 66,* 102294. https://doi.org/10.1016/j.healthplace.2020.102294

Organisation for Economic Co-operation and Development (OECD). (2018). *Gender equality.* https://www.oecd.org/en/topics/policy-issues/gender-equality.html

Palmer, R. (2017). *Jobs and skills mismatch in the informal economy.* International Labour Organization. May 2018. https://www.ilo.org/sites/default/files/wcmsp5/groups/public/@ed_emp/@ifp_skills/documents/publication/wcms_629018.pdf

Pan American Health Organization (PAHO). (2018). *Gender equality in health.* https://www.paho.org/en/topics/gender-equality-health

Pei, A. (2021, October 7). *5 environmental benefits of sustainable transportation | UCLA transportation.* 5 Environmental Benefits of Sustainable Transportation. https://transportation.ucla.edu/blog/5-environmental-benefits-sustainable-transportation

Pearce, D., & Standing, G. (2001). *Globalisation, growth and inequality: Demonstrating a 'poverty bias' in world trade*. United Nations Development Programme.

Petrova, S., & Simcock, N. (2021). Gender and energy: Domestic inequities reconsidered. *Social and Cultural Geography, 22*(6), 849–867. https://doi.org/10.1080/14649365.2019.1645200

Philipp, J. (2023, May 18). *The state of renewable energy in Jamaica*. The Borgen Project. https://borgenproject.org/renewable-energy-in-jamaica/

PIOJ. (2022). *GOAL 7: Ensure access to affordable, reliable, sustainable and modern energy for all*. https://www.pioj.gov.jm/wp-content/uploads/2022/10/VNR_Goal_7.pdf

Pietrapertosa, F., Tancredi, M., Giordano, M., Cosmi, C., & Salvia, M. (2021). How to prioritize energy efficiency interventions in municipal public buildings to decrease CO_2 emissions? A case study from Italy. *International Journal of Environmental Research and Public Health, 18*(7), 3760. https://doi.org/10.3390/ijerph18073760 PubMed

Planning Institute of Jamaica. (2009, June). *Natural resources and environmental management sector plan*. Vision 2030 Jamaica. https://www.vision2030.gov.jm/wpcontent/uploads/sites/2/2020/12/Microsoft-Word-Natural-Resources-and-Environmental-Managment-June-2009.pdf

Planning Institute of Jamaica. (2022). *Gender assessment study: Final report*. https://www.pioj.gov.jm/product/gender-assessment-study-final-report/

Planning Institute of Jamaica. (2022). *Message from the Director-General*. https://www.vision2030.gov.jm/blog/message-from-the-director-general-planning-institute-of-jamaicapioj/vision2030.gov.jm

Planning Institute of Jamaica (PIOJ) & Statistical Institute of Jamaica (STATIN). (2018). *The report on the Jamaica Survey of Establishments 2018*. https://www.pioj.gov.jm/product/the-report-on-the-jamaica-survey-of-establishments-2018-3/

Policy Planning Development and Evaluation Division, Research Unit. (2018). *Title of the work*. Ministry of Science, Energy, Telecommunications and Transport. mset.gov.jm

Powell, L. (2016). Energy transition in a carbon consuming country: India. In R. Looney (Ed.), *Handbook of transitions to energy and climate security* (pp. 259–272). Routledge.

Promoting energy justice. (n.d.). Energy.gov. https://www.energy.gov/promoting-energy-justice

Reddy, A. K. N. (2000). Energy and social issues. In J. Goldemberg (Ed.), *World Energy Assessment: Energy and the Challenge of Sustainability* (pp. 39–60). United Nations Development Programme.

Reddy, A. K. N., & Reddy, B. S. (1994). Subsidies and sustainable development: Key issues. *Energy for Sustainable Development, 1*(1), 17–24.

Renewable Energy Systems Training (REST). (2022). *K-12 Renewable Energy Workshop: Lecture Slides*. https://ate.is/index.php?ID=42314&P=FullRecord

Rengasamy, S., et al. (2001). *Thaan Vuzha Nilam Tharisu – The land without a farmer becomes barren: Policies that work for sustainable agriculture and rural livelihoods in Virudhunagar District, Tamil Nadu*. International Institute for Environment and Development (IIED).

Richards, D., & Yabar, H. (2022). Potential of renewable energy in Jamaica's power sector: Feasibility analysis of biogas production for electricity generation. *Sustainability, 14*(11), 6457. https://doi.org/10.3390/su14116457IDEAS/RePEc

Ritchie, C. (2024, February 2). *Women in the energy industry*. SaveOnEnergy.com. https://www.saveonenergy.com/resources/women-in-energy/

Robertson, K. (2023, January 10). *Mia Mottley: Caribbean, or World leader?* Americas Quarterly. https://www.americasquarterly.org/article/mia-mottley-caribbean-or-world-leader/#:~:text=Mottley%2C%2057%2C%20has%20become%20a,attention%20to%20her%20outspoken%20style

Robeyns, I. (2016, October 3). *The capability approach*. Stanford Encyclopedia of Philosophy. https://plato.stanford.edu/archIves/sum2020/entries/capability-approach/

Robinson, C. (2019). Energy poverty and gender in England: A spatial perspective. *Geoforum, 104*, 222–233. https://doi.org/10.1016/j.geoforum.2019.05.001

Rodgers, Y. v. d. M. (2022). Time poverty: Conceptualization, gender differences, and policy implications. *Social Philosophy & Policy*, forthcoming.

Rose, D. (2024). *Wigton accelerating diversification: Shareholders to vote on name change as company eyes opportunities away from wind*. Jamaica Observer. https://www.jamaicaobserver.com/

Roshan, D., & Isaifan, R. (2018). Household air pollution from burning biomass for cooking and heating – A review of health hazards and intervention programs. *Journal of Environmental Science and Pollution Research, 4*, 289–296. https://doi.org/10.30799/jespr.139.18040302

Samarakoon, S. (2019). 'A justice and wellbeing centered framework for analysing energy poverty in the Global South'. *Ecological Economics, 165*, p. 106385. https://doi.org/10.1016/J.ECOLECON.2019.106385

Sánchez-Guevara Sánchez, C., Sanz Fernández, A., & Núñez Peiró, M. (2020). Feminisation of energy poverty in the city of Madrid. *Energy and Buildings, 223*, 110157. https://doi.org/10.1016/j.enbuild.2019.110157

Saner, R., & Yiu, L. (2019). Jamaica's development of women entrepreneurship: Challenges and opportunities. *Public Administration and Policy: An Asia-Pacific Journal, 22*(2), 152–172. https://doi.org/10.1108/PAP-09-2019-0023

Sangha, P. S., Thakur, M., Akhtar, Z., Ramani, S., & Gyamfi, R. S. (2020). The link between rheumatoid arthritis and dementia: A review. *Cureus, 12*(4), e7855. https://doi.org/10.7759/cureus.7855. PMID: 32489719; PMCID: PMC7255531.

Satz, D. (2013, October 21). *Feminist perspectives on reproduction and the family.* Stanford Encyclopedia of Philosophy. https://plato.stanford.edu/entries/feminism-

Sen, A. (2001). *Development as freedom.* Oxford University Press.

Sign, D., & Ru, X. (2022). Gender and energy: Exploring the intersection of gender and energy access. *Energy Research & Social Science, 87*, 102541. https://doi.org/10.1016/j.erss.2022.102541

Small, S. (2024, November 22). *Wolmer's group of Schools Reaps Big Savings from solar panels.* Lead Stories | Jamaica Gleaner. https://jamaica-gleaner.com/article/lead-stories/20241122/wolmers-group-schools-reaps-big-savings-solar-panels

Smart Energy. (n.d.). *Educational options in energy will lead to a brighter future for Barbadians.* https://smartenergybarbados.com/press-releases/educational-options-in-energy-will-lead-to-a-brighter-future-for-barbadians/

Smelser, N. J., & Baltes, P. B. (Eds.). (2001). *International encyclopedia of the social & behavioral sciences.* Elsevier.

Smith, L. C., & Haddad, L. (2015). Reducing child undernutrition: Past drivers and priorities for the post-MDG era. *World Development, 68*, 180–204. https://www.sciencedirect.com/science/article/pii/S0305750X14003834

Spiegel, S., & Schwank, O. (2022, May 27). *Bridging the "great finance divide" in developing countries.* Brookings. https://www.brookings.edu/articles/bridging-the-great-finance-divide-in-developing-countries/

Srivastav Energy Economist, S. (2022, April 12). *How clean energy can empower women in rural communities.* International Growth Centre. https://www.theigc.org/blogs/gender-equality/how-clean-energy-can-empower-women-rural-communities

Stanford Encyclopedia of Philosophy. (2004). *Feminist perspectives on reproduction and the family.* https://plato.stanford.edu/entries/feminism-family/

Statistical Institute of Jamaica, Inter-American Development Bank, & UN Women. (2018). *Women's Health Survey 2016: Jamaica—Summary Report.* https://caribbean.unwomen.org/sites/default/files/Field%20Office%20Caribbean/Attachments/Publications/2018/20181012%20AF%20Jamaica%20Summary%20for%20digital.pdf

Statista Research Department. (2023, September 12). *Homicide rate in Latin America by country.* Statista. https://www.statista.com/statistics/947781/homicide-rates-latin-america-caribbean-country/

Sunrun. (n.d.). *How renewable energy can help low income communities.* https://www.sunrun.com/go-solar-center/renewable-energy-helps-low-income-communities

The CLEAN Network. (2013). *The quality of life of individuals and societies is affected by energy choices.* https://cleanet.org/clean/literacy/energy7.html

The Gleaner. (2014, December 1). *Women continue to head most Jamaican families with children.* https://jamaica-gleaner.com/power/56947JamaicaGleaner

The Gleaner. (2023). *JPS makes record profit from summer.* https://jamaica-gleaner.com/article/business/20230915/jps-makes-record-profit-summer

UN Women. (2015). *Gender equality, women's empowerment and climate change.* https://www.unwomen.org/en/news/in-focus/climate-change/2015

United Nations. (2021). *The Sustainable Development Goals Report 2021.* United Nations. https://unstats.un.org/sdgs/report/2021/The-Sustainable-Development-Goals-Report-2021.pdf

United Nations. (2022). *The Sustainable Development Goals Report 2022.* United Nations. https://unstats.un.org/sdgs/report/2022/The-Sustainable-Development-Goals-Report-2022.pdf

UNDP. (n.d.). *Energy and gender equality.* https://www.undp.org/energy/our-work-areas/energy-and-gender-equality

UNICEF. (2007). *The state of the world's children 2007: Women and children—the double dividend of gender equality.* https://www.unicef.org/reports/state-worlds-children-2007

United Nations. (n.d.). *Good governance in sustainable development | department of economic and social affairs.* United Nations. https://sdgs.un.org/partnerships/good-governance-sustainable-development#:~:text=The%20objective%20of%20Good%20Governance,development%20principles%20through%20global%20partnership.

United Nations Development Programme (UNDP). (n.d.). *Transforming the future of work for gender equality initiative.* https://jobs.undp.org/cj_view_job.cfm?job_id=88905

United Nations Development Programme (UNDP). (2021). *EnGenDER Highlights.* https://www.undp.org/barbados/engender-highlights

United Nations Development Programme (UNDP). (2022). *EnGenDER Highlights.* https://www.undp.org/barbados/engender-highlights

United Nations Educational, Scientific and Cultural Organization (UNESCO). (2019). *Gender equality.* [Details not specified].

United Nations Department of Economic and Social Affairs. (2023). *The Sustainable Development Goals Report 2023: Special Edition.* United Nations. https://unstats.un.org/sdgs/report/2023/

United Nations Development Programme. (2017). *Breaking up with fossil fuels.* Retrieved May 11, 2025, from https://featured.undp.org/breaking-up-with-fossil-fuels/

United Nations Economic Commission for Latin America and the Caribbean (ECLAC). (2021). *Implications of gender roles in natural resource governance in Latin America and the Caribbean.* https://www.cepal.org/en/insights/implications-gender-roles-natural-resource-governance-latin-america-andcaribbean

University of Sussex. (2021). *What is energy justice?* https://study-online.sussex.ac.uk/news-and-events/what-isenergy-justice/

U.S. Agency for International Development. (2017). *USAID report to Congress on health-related research and development for fiscal year 2017.* https://www.usaid.gov/document/usaid-report-congress-health-related-research-and-development-fiscal-year-2017 USAID

U.S. Energy Information Administration - EIA - independent statistics and analysis. (2022, December 27). Wind energy and the environment - U.S. Energy Information Administration (EIA). https://www.eia.gov/energyexplained/wind/wind-energy-and-the-environment.php

U.S. Department of Energy. (n.d.). *Low-Income Energy Affordability Data (LEAD) Tool.* https://www.energy.gov/indianenergy/low-income-energy-affordability-data-lead-tool

U.S. Department of Energy, Office of Energy Efficiency & Renewable Energy. (n.d.). *About the Office of Energy Efficiency & Renewable Energy.* Retrieved May 11, 2025, from https://www.energy.gov/eere/about-office-energy-efficiency-and-renewable-energy

Verma, A. (2023). Promoting energy and resource recovery from livestock waste. *Journal of Environmental Management, 325,* 116389. https://doi.org/10.1016/j.jenvman.2022.116389 ScienceDirect+1ScienceDirect+1

Watson Williams, C. (2018). Jamaica women's health survey 2016: Final report. Inter-American Development Bank & UN Women. https://doi.org/10.18235/0001170

What is feminist political ecology (FPE)? - wego-ITN. (2020, May 19). WEGO. https://www.wegoitn.org/online-learning/what-is-feminist-political-ecology-fpe/

William, R. (2021, March 15). *Leveraging energy from renewable sources key to creating new Jamaica.* Jamaica Information Services. https://jis.gov.jm/leveraging-energy-from-renewable-sources-key-to-creating-new-jamaica-minister-vaz/

Williams, G. A. (2006). *An evaluation of the low-income housing sector in Jamaica.* (Master's thesis). Georgia Institute of Technology.

Winkler, H., et al. (2011). Access and affordability of electricity in developing countries. *World Development, 39*(6), 1037–1050.

Wohlgemuth, N. (2023). Decentralized power generation: Community microgrids with ocean energy. *Renewable and Sustainable Energy Reviews, 159,* 112203. https://doi.org/10.1016/j.rser.2022.112203

World Bank. (1996). *Rural energy and development: Improving energy supplies for two billion people*. World Bank Development in Practice.

World Bank. (2010). *Education and health services in Latin America: The impact of women's education on child health*. documents.worldbank.org/en/publication/documents-reports/documentdetail/884161468270311328/education-and-health-services-in-latin-america-the-impact-of-womens-education-on-child-health

World Bank Group. (2015, August 3). *In Rwanda, a brighter future for Miriam*. World Bank. https://www.worldbank.org/en/news/feature/2015/03/05/in-rwanda-a-brighter-future-for-miriam

World Bank Group. (2019, April 26). *Improving energy efficiency and security in Jamaica*. Results Briefs. https://www.worldbank.org/en/results/2019/04/26/improving-energy-efficiency-and-security-in-jamaica

World Bank Group. (2024). *Results and performance of the World Bank Group 2024: Managing results in an uncertain world*. https://documents.worldbank.org/en/publication/documents-reports/documentdetail/099841003072529467/secbos11faeefa037180061e7fc55ee14ed World Bank

World Economic Forum. (2022). *Annual report 2021–2022*. https://www.weforum.org/publications/annual-report-2021-2022/ World Economic Forum+1World Economic Forum+1

World Health Organization (WHO). (2018). *Gender equality in health*. https://www.paho.org/en/topics/gender-equality-health

World Health Organization. (2019). *World health statistics 2019: Monitoring health for the SDGs*. https://www.who.int/publications/i/item/9789241565707 World Health Organization (WHO)

World Health Organization (WHO). (2021). *Household air pollution and health*. https://www.who.int/news-room/fact-sheets/detail/household-air-pollution-and-health

World Health Organization (WHO). (2023). *Household air pollution and health*. [Details not specified].

World Health Organization. (2024, May 7). *WHO Results Report 2023 shows notable health achievements and calls for concerted drive toward Sustainable Development Goals*. https://www.who.int/news/item/07-05-2024-who-results-report-2023-shows-notable-health-achievements-and-calls-for-concerted-drive-toward-sustainable-development-goals

World Health Organization (WHO) & United Nations Children's Fund (UNICEF). (2021). *Billions of people will lack access to safe water, sanitation and hygiene in 2030 unless progress quadruples*. https://armenia.un.org/en/134619-billions-people-will-lack-access-safe-water-sanitation-and-hygiene-2030-unlessprogress

Worldometer. (2023). *World population clock*. https://www.worldometers.info/world-population/

Xiao, Y., Wu, H., Wang, G., & Wang, S. (2021). The relationship between energy poverty and individual development: Exploring the serial mediating effects of learning behavior and health condition. *International Journal of Environmental Research and Public Health*, *18*(16), 8888. https://doi.org/10.3390/ijerph18168888. PMID: 34444636; PMCID: PMC8393606.

Yabar, H., Nhiakao, K., & Mizunoya, T. (2022). Cost-benefit analysis of the Nam Che 1 hydropower plant, Thathom District, Laos: An ex-post analysis. *Sustainability*, *14*(6), 3178. https://doi.org/10.3390/su14063178

YW Boston Blog. (2017, March 29). *What is intersectionality, and what does it have to do with me?*. https://www.ywboston.org/2017/03/what-is-intersectionality-and-what-does-it-have-to-do-with-me/

Index

A
Access to renewable energy, 120
Affordable energy solutions, 121
Alternative energy financing, 115
Awareness campaigns for energy access, 112

B
Barriers to energy access for women, 31
Benefits of decentralized energy systems, 109
Biomass energy, 19
Business opportunities for women in energy, 82

C
Capacity building for women in energy, 38, 59
Care economy, 3–5

Caribbean energy solutions, 17, 58, 76–77, 79, 80, 83–87, 113, 116–117, 124
Clean cooking technologies, 48
Climate change
   impacts on energy poverty, 47–49, 52, 91
   in communities, 6–7
Community-based renewable energy, 60, 108
Community development, 20–21, 104
Cost of energy systems, 108
Cultural
   barriers to energy equity, 31
   factors, 3

D
Decentralized energy systems, 71–73, 108–110
Development goals and energy access, 93

INDEX

Disabled women, 94–95
Displacement and energy poverty, 105–123

E
Ecofeminism, 36–37
Economic empowerment, 6, 11, 54, 59
Economic opportunities, 16, 20, 21, 42, 54, 56, 67, 94–96
Education and energy poverty, 42, 46, 53
Electricity access for women, 5, 6, 22, 30, 42
Energy
  affordability, 77
  cooperatives, 72
  democracy, 38–39
  efficiency initiatives, 126
  governance, 38, 73, 109
  infrastructure in low-income communities, 77
  justice, 30–31, 73, 109
  plan, 57
  policy development, 59, 70, 108, 112, 118
  poverty, 2–22, 28, 30, 38, 42–60, 71–73, 76–96, 103, 106, 108–110, 114
  poverty and the environment, 16, 18–20, 91
  subsidies, 59, 69, 107, 125
  transition, 30, 36, 45, 107
Environmental impacts of energy poverty, 16, 18, 86, 92

F
Female business, 35, 82–84
Female headed household, 21, 78, 82–83

Feminisation of poverty, 3, 20
Feminist political ecology, 29–30
Financing renewable energy, 2, 44, 59, 110, 116, 125
Fossil fuel dependency and women, 55, 67, 86, 88, 122

G
Gender
  and development theory, 31–33
  disparities in energy access, 5, 6, 110
  and electricity in communities, 5–6, 22
  and energy, 2–22, 28, 76–96
  equity, 42, 54–60
  mainstreaming in energy policies, 32, 70, 71
  roles, 34, 42, 51, 71, 77–82, 91
Gender-based energy strategies, 36
Global finance, 44–45
Global perspective, 42–44
Governance of energy systems, 73
Grid-connected energy, 56–57

H
Health impacts of energy poverty, 18, 42, 52–53, 94, 95
Household energy management, 46
Hydropower plants, 55

I
Inclusive energy solutions, 110
Income generation through energy access, 109
Inequalities in energy access, 4, 58, 92
Innovations in renewable energy, 59, 110, 121, 122
Innovative technologies, 45–46
Institutional Reforms, 58–59

J

Jamaica, v, 2, 5, 7–8, 12–15, 18, 22, 30–34, 44, 48, 54–58, 60, 66–68, 71–73, 77–79, 83, 87–93, 102, 103, 106, 108–110, 112, 113, 116, 118–120, 122–127
Jamaica Public Service (JPS), 56, 58, 68, 87–90, 119, 125, 127

L

Localized energy systems, 109, 110
Long-term impacts of energy access, 67
Low income communities, v, 2

M

Minority women, 51

P

Participatory approaches, 35–36, 38
Policy gaps in energy equity, 59–60
Productive uses of energy, 68
Public-private partnerships, 59–60, 104, 107, 113

R

Regulation and standards, 102, 111, 116–120
Renewable energy
 adoption, 106, 119, 126
 education programmes, 59, 112
Role of women in energy solutions, 8
Rural electrification, 12

S

Single sex household, 2
Social
 equity in energy access, 59, 110
 factors, 118
 reproduction theory, 33–34
Solar energy systems, 103, 104, 122
Stakeholders, 28, 42, 106, 110, 124–126
Sustainable energy solutions, 38
Sustainable livelihoods through energy, 28, 69

T

Technology adoption and diffusion theory, 34–35
Time savings from energy access, 54
Training programmes for women in energy, 38, 59

W

Wind energy, 55, 56, 107
Women
 empowerment through energy, 54, 59, 70
 globally, 46–52
 health and energy access, 50, 52, 53
 participation in energy governance, 73, 109
Women-led energy businesses, 84
Workforce development in renewable energy for women, 105, 112

Y

Young women, 59, 93–94

9783031890789